What puts a football team on the fiᵥ West Virginia, a town full of Beaver Believers? A boy with a ball, leaping every hurdle, takes you to the dawn runs, clashes in practice and underdog upsets that turn tempestuous teens into a championship team. A state title won in the nation's top high school football stadium, a field of dreams for Donnie Jackson, will make you a Beaver Believer.

— **Ran Henry**, writing professor at the University of Virginia, author of the definitive biography *Spurrier: How the Ball Coach Taught the South to Play Football*, and *All God's Children: How Clementa Pinckney Transformed the Confederacy.*

In this heartfelt memoir, written by one of Bluefield's former star running backs, Donnie Jackson shares the story of fulfilling his childhood dream of playing football for the Bluefield High School Beavers while also telling, in spell-binding detail, game action from the 1973 to 1975 seasons. With humor and humility, he weaves a superb human-interest story of high school gridiron competition evoking memories of *Hoosiers* and other memorable sports stories. This book contains a wealth of information about Bluefield High School football in the 1960s and '70s and is an entertaining read. It takes you back to small-town America and has you pulling for Donnie and his fellow Beavers.

— **Harriet E. Michael**, award winning author and freelance writer, 2021 Selah Award Winner.

An engaging inside look at one of the most successful high school football programs in West Virginia history. Donnie Jackson was intelligent, athletic, and determined to win! I am proud to have been a small part of his playing career.

— **Coach Chuck Martin**, former football coach at Bluefield, Vance, Jacksonville, and Laney high schools, Marshall University, University of North Carolina, and Ohio University.

MAROON & WHITE

My Story of
Bluefield Beavers Football
Donald K. Jackson

Gallery Place
Press

Maroon &White
© 2021 Donald K. Jackson

ISBN: 978-1-7375359-0-4

All photos are property of the author or published with permission from owners. Sources include the *Bluefield Daily Telegraph* and the 1975 Beaver football program.

This book is a memoir and by definition represents the author's present recollections of experience in the past. No names have been changed or omitted on purpose. Some events have been compressed and are subject to the perspective of the author.

On the cover: *Headed for the endzone in state title game with Joe Hager, #66, blocking.*
Interior and cover design by Faith Driven Book Productions.

Printed in the United States.

Dedication

For my family, friends,

and fans of high school football.

Contents

When the Bluefield Beavers won their second state title in 1962, my dad took me to the game at Laidley Field in Charleston, West Virginia. I was only four years old, but I clearly understood Bluefield had won "a big game" by defeating Parkersburg 40–12. After the 1962 season, I don't recall ever missing a home football game for the next thirteen years. I played in many of them, proudly wearing the school's colors—

MAROON & WHITE.

Preface

I must begin by saying I did not initially set out to write a published memoir. About twenty years after graduating from high school, I read an article asserting anyone who wished to write an autobiography or family history should start doing so when that person was old enough to reflect on the past, but young enough to recall events. At age forty, I decided to write my story for my family. I wrote much of the draft and then put it away. Occasionally, I would add to the story, make revisions, and then put it away again.

Then in 2019, Harriet Edwards Michael, my friend and former classmate who is now an author, mentioned to me an idea of a novel about our shared high school experiences including the excitement around our football team. I informed her I had already written much of that story since my story is deeply intertwined with the story of Bluefield High School football. With Harriet's encouragement, I finished my memoir and shared it with her. From that point forward, she has been an invaluable resource to me with her content editing, suggestions, and introductions to the publishing community. This memoir would not have been published without her guidance and support.

I would like to thank all the coaches, players, and fans who helped build the legacy of Bluefield Beavers football over the past six decades under the leadership of head coaches Merrill Gainer, John Chmara, and Fred Simon. A special thanks goes to my coaches and teammates from the 1973 to 1975 seasons.

Typical of anyone writing a memoir, I relied heavily on my memory of events. To supplement my recollections, I relied on sports articles from that period in the Bluefield Daily Telegraph. Although the newspaper served an area represented by at least a couple dozen high schools, the head sportswriter, Virgil L. "Stubby" Currence was unabashedly first and foremost a supporter of the Beavers, hence his reporting contained a wealth of information about Bluefield football from that era. I also watched copies of game films provided to me by my former teammate, Randy Albert, as a reminder of what took place.

In addition to Harriet, I would like to thank Ran Henry and Coach Chuck Martin for their endorsements. Ran also provided sound advice to me in how to approach writing this story.

Thanks to René Holt, for her professional copy editing, and to Marji Laine Clubine for her assistance in cover design and publishing.

Of course, I owe much gratitude to my parents, Kenneth and Jane, who walked each step of my journey with me, as did my sisters, Ann and Sandy.

Finally, I would like to thank my wife, Nancy, and our three children, Keith, Kelly, and Ken, for reading my drafts and inspiring me to finish my story. I trust one day my grandchildren will read this book and understand I was once young too.

I hope fans of Bluefield Beavers football, and high school football fans in general, will enjoy reading my story and appreciate the special relationship of one small town with its beloved football team.

Chapter One

Bluefield
An All-American City

This is a story about a small town in southern West Virginia with a passion for its high school football team, the Bluefield Beavers. During my childhood, the team developed into one of the most prominent football programs in the state. This is also the story of how I came to play a role in continuing that tradition and fulfilling my childhood dream.

In the 1960s, Bluefield embodied the spirit of quintessential small-town America. Nestled on the western edge of East River Mountain in the Appalachian mountain range, Bluefield provided pretty much everything I wanted as a kid growing up. The state border, separating the two Virginias, runs northeast along the ridge of East River Mountain. The state line also runs perpendicular to East River Mountain, separating the towns of Bluefield, West Virginia and Bluefield, Virginia. Due to its elevation, Bluefield rarely experienced summer days exceeding ninety degrees. In fact, when the temperature exceeded ninety degrees, the Bluefield Chamber of Commerce served free lemonade to anyone who happened to be downtown. Because of this temperate climate, Bluefield promoted itself as "Nature's Air-conditioned City." Autumn ushered in cooler weather, and winter brought frequent snow. The area acquired the nickname "Four Seasons Country" because each of the four seasons are equally represented.

In 1964 Bluefield was designated an "All-American City" as evidenced by the billboards scattered throughout town. I have no idea how it received that honor or how many other towns in America also received that designation. It was irrelevant. For the people of Bluefield, being an All-American City constituted a source of pride. As a young boy, I considered Bluefield a special place. Although its population included less than twenty thousand citizens, Bluefield was one of the larger cities in West Virginia. The greater Bluefield area, including Bluefield, Virginia, and small communities outside the city limits, pushed the population close to forty thousand at that time.

In those days, downtown bustled with activity. Many people, including my dad, worked downtown. Others in the Bluefield area commuted about an hour each way into the nearby coal mines. Although Bluefield does not reside in the coal fields, it operated as a main gateway and center for transporting coal out of the area via the Norfolk and Western railroad. According to historians, the N&W railroad had fueled Bluefield's growth during the first half of the twentieth century. The rest of the country relied heavily on coal from the region to support the Industrial Revolution. Unfortunately for the region, with the increase of alternative fuels and global sources, the demand for coal started to recede in the second half of the century.

Downtown Bluefield consisted of a main road flanked on either side by office buildings, stores, and shops of all sorts. Like many families, we frequented downtown often—to purchase clothes, shoes, see a movie at one of the two movie theatres, or just visit my dad at work. The hospital, called the Bluefield Sanitarium, along with numerous doctor and dentist offices, resided close to the center of downtown, so healthcare issues also required a trip into town. Bluefield offered a variety of dining options including sit-down restaurants, drive-thru burger places, and pizza joints. Nothing fancy, but more than sufficient for me. I also enjoyed the numerous varieties of milkshakes at the local ice cream places, including a drive-in where the servers brought the ice cream right up to the car window. In short, Bluefield possessed all the charm and character one would expect of an "All-American City."

However, in the 1960s, Bluefield became known for one more thing … winning high school football games. For a significant portion of Bluefield's citizens, high school football gave the town a source of pride and identity.

Beaver Football

In 1959, Coach Merrill Gainer came to Bluefield from Big Creek High School in War, West Virginia. He had already developed a reputation as a winning high school coach, and he lived up to his reputation right away when he proceeded to win the Bluefield Beavers' first AAA state championship by defeating

Parkersburg 19–13. Obviously, as an eighteen-month-old toddler at the time, I have no recollection of that first state championship. I should clarify the terms Bluefield football and Beaver football were used interchangeably since the current Bluefield High School was originally named Beaver High School.

However, when the Bluefield Beavers won their second state title in 1962, my dad took me to the game at Laidley Field in Charleston, West Virginia. I was only four years old, but I clearly understood Bluefield had won "a big game" by defeating Parkersburg 40–12. After the 1962 season, I don't recall ever missing a home football game for the next thirteen years. I played in many of them, proudly wearing the school's colors—maroon and white. I was not alone. Many supporters never missed a home game.

Bluefield's home field, Mitchell Stadium, seated ten thousand people. Built by the Works Progress Administration in 1936, the stadium was named in honor of Emory Mitchell in 1954. Mitchell had been the city manager who spearheaded the effort to build the football stadium as well as the nearby baseball field and city park. Located on the state line, Mitchell Stadium served as the home field for both Bluefield High School, in Bluefield, West Virginia, and Graham High School, in Bluefield, Virginia.

When Bluefield played an opponent from a nearby school, like Graham or Princeton, the stadium was always packed. Once the season started, on Fridays I spent a good deal of my day anxiously awaiting that night's game. When the weather turned colder, my mom would make hot chocolate for our family after the game. Drinking hot chocolate on cold Friday nights remains a favorite childhood memory.

Bluefield won another state title in 1965, led by quarterback Dickie Ward, running back Pete Wood, and a great defense. The 1965 team outscored its regular season opponents by a cumulative score of 305–19 and then defeated Dunbar High School 13–0 in the championship game at Laidley Field in Charleston. My dad once again took me to the game which I better understood as a seven-year-old.

Most people who followed Beaver football expected the 1966 team to be even better than the 1965 team with Dickie Ward, Pete Wood, Johnny Beckett, and several other returning starters. However, a loss away from home to Coach Gainer's former school, Big Creek, blemished that team's record. I listened to the 1966 Big Creek game on the radio. Bluefield's WHIS radio station carried all the Beavers' games, home and away. Even though Bluefield finished the season with a 9–1 record, there would be no repeat state championship. In those days, a team needed to finish the regular season ranked as one of the top two teams in the state to qualify for the state championship game. That left no margin for error. One loss generally knocked a team out of the two-team playoff. The state rankings were determined entirely using a mathematical formula with teams earning points based on its wins and strength-of-schedule. The strength-of-schedule factored in the number of wins by a team's opponents. For example, defeating a team that ended the season with an 8–2 record carried far more weight than defeating a team with a 2–8 record.

Returning to undefeated status, the 1967 team, led by Pete Sarver, Ronnie Goodwin, and Jimmy Beckett, won the AAA state championship by defeating Stonewall Jackson of Charleston 27–7 in Parkersburg. That team outscored its regular season opponents 305–32. However, the 1967 season marked the end of Merrill Gainer's coaching career at Bluefield. He decided to move on to another job in Roanoke, Virginia. From 1959 to 1967, Coach Gainer amassed a record of 87–6–1 with three of the six losses occurring in 1963.

My eventual head coach, John Chmara, took over the program in 1968 and finished his first season undefeated at 9–0. However, due to the point system in place, the undefeated 1968 team ended the season ranked third in the state and did not qualify for the state championship game. At that time, I could not comprehend how the best team in the state, at least in my opinion, would not even get a chance to play for the title. From 1969 to 1971, Coach Chmara's teams posted a cumulative record of 21–7–1. Bluefield failed to qualify for the playoffs during that three-year stretch by losing at least two games in each of those three seasons. In 1972, the state athletic association expanded the playoffs from two teams to four teams. Had that been the rule in 1968, the undefeated Beavers would have made the playoffs, but it was too little and too late for the '68 team.

Perhaps appropriately, Bluefield benefitted from the first year of the expanded format and returned to the playoffs in 1972. Ranked third after finishing the regular season 10–0, Bluefield faced second ranked Dupont in a semifinal game. Playing again at Laidley Field in Charleston, the Beavers lost to Dupont 34–32 in double overtime. I watched that game under gray skies and felt such a letdown when it ended. It was the first time I had experienced Bluefield losing a playoff game. On the positive side, the 1972 team featured several juniors in key positions who would be returning in 1973—my first year at Bluefield High. Despite the disappointing semifinal loss, I assumed the 1973 team would be a cinch to return to the playoffs.

I grew up in a time that encompassed some of the most impactful years of the twentieth century. I recall the assassinations of John F. Kennedy, Dr. Martin Luther King, Jr., and Bobby Kennedy. The Vietnam War, war protests, the Civil Rights movement, the Cold War, and the race to the moon headlined the nightly news. I appreciated the significance of all those events. However, being tucked away in my own small corner of the world, the thing that mattered most to me was the success of Beaver football and my hopes to one day be a part of the team.

Chapter Two

The Early Years
Elementary School, 1964–1970

My days as a Bluefield Beaver began in 1973, but here is a little background about my life, especially my football life prior to high school. I attended Brushfork Elementary School starting in 1964. Brushfork is located about one mile north of Harry Heights, where I lived with my parents, Kenneth and Jane, and my two sisters, Ann and Sandy. Our school bus ride lasted all of two minutes. Students in grades one through six who lived north of the Bluefield city limits and south of the unincorporated town of Bluewell, were zoned to attend Brushfork. The school consisted of one class for each of the six grade levels with roughly twenty students per class. When I started school, I had no idea how I would perform academically compared to other students. No one in my class had attended pre-school. During the first few days, I struggled with many of the lessons. Oh great! I thought school was going to be a disaster.

However, after a short period of time, things seemed to click. Suddenly, I started to easily comprehend math, reading, spelling, and any other subject the teacher introduced. I began to view academics as a competition that I wanted to win. Fortunately, I learned new concepts quickly. Being a quick learner benefitted me greatly throughout my school days. It allowed me to devote more time to athletics and still make good grades. In fact, I learned so quickly my teachers wanted me to skip a grade and join the class one year ahead of me.

My dad said, "Absolutely not!"

Dad had started school as a five-year-old, then skipped a grade in elementary school. As a result, he graduated from high school at the age of sixteen. Being two years younger than his classmates diminished his chances to participate in organized sports. Thankfully, he ensured I avoided that problem.

I attended twelve years of school with many of the boys and girls I met in first grade. Of course, many of my good friends in elementary school became casual friends in junior high and simply acquaintances by the time we reached high school.

We had three breaks each day for what I considered one of the highlights of elementary school—recess period. Our breaks were spaced out so that we had one at mid-morning, one immediately after lunch, and one at mid-afternoon. Students in grades one through three had recess at a small field behind the school. I have few memories from that field. Students in grades four through six went to a larger field in front of the school. One area of the field was used for kickball, one area for football, and another area for simply hanging out and passing time until recess ended. Along with most of my friends, I played football at every opportunity. We started the first recess period each day by choosing sides for the two teams. The game and the score carried over from recess to recess until the final bell sounded at the conclusion of afternoon recess. We always played tackle football, not touch, so of course our clothes stayed dirty throughout the day. In addition, a small creek that smelled of sewage comprised the boundary of one sideline. Occasionally, someone would get tackled or knocked into the creek. Whenever this happened, our teacher would complain about us playing football and would tell us we should play touch football, instead. Not a chance.

After returning home from school in the afternoons, my friends and I would meet to play more football, or perhaps basketball. Regardless of the sport, the teams usually consisted of two players per side since four boys around my age lived in Harry Heights. Our neighborhood gang consisted of Steve Dalton, who was one grade ahead of me, Brent Sizemore, who was one grade behind me, and Charlie Woods who was two grades behind. Steve's younger brother, Timothy, played with us occasionally as he got older. Most of the time, the teams consisted of Charlie and me against Steve and Brent.

We played football in our yards or a small vacant lot close to my house. If we chose to play basketball, we used a dirt basketball court in my neighbor's back yard. When it rained, the ball would get caked with mud, making it difficult to shoot but much more entertaining. When I was about ten, some neighbors put up a basketball goal in their paved driveway for their nephew who visited them on weekends. They had no children of their own.

Their driveway became the basketball court of choice. However, my friends and I would continue to play in their driveway even after the husband came home from work and parked in the driveway. We simply viewed the car as an obstacle to be avoided and we tried to make sure the ball did not bounce off the car too often. As you might suspect, our neighbors soon took down the goal, so we went back to playing football.

My dad's youngest brother, Jack, was only a few years older than me. Jack taught me football skills in the front yard of my grandmother's house. In the fall, he would create a small football field by raking leaves to clear the grass and fashion the boundaries with colorful maple and oak leaves. Then we took turns giving each other one play to score. Since he was bigger than me, I could not tackle him. But when it was my turn to run the ball, Jack showed me tips on how to avoid tackles, keep my balance, and spin after contact—skills that would later define my running style. During one of our games, I fell on a large rock bordering the field and sustained a hairline fracture of my right collarbone, ending the lessons as Jack never wanted to risk injuring me again.

Organized football

I first played organized football in 1967 when I entered the fourth grade. The Pee Wee league consisted of four teams. I played for the American Legion. The players on that team came from the north side of town, home to a substantial part of the black population of Bluefield. Although I always played running back during recess at Brushfork, the coach moved me to offensive guard from day one of practice. I guess after looking over the players, he perceived he had better options to carry the football. I can barely remember my first year of football. I think we played two games.

However, things changed in the fifth grade when a young coach named Jeffries, a part-time helper at the start of fall practice, moved me to fullback. We were doing a drill called "bull in the ring" in which a ball carrier (the bull) stood in the middle of a circle of players (the ring). The coach then called out one or more players from the circle to tackle the ball carrier. When it was my turn to be the bull, Coach Jeffries liked my ability to fight off tacklers, so he moved me from offensive guard to fullback. Our star player that year was a sixth-grade halfback named Charles Thomas, or "Baby Charles," as most people called him. He scored most of our touchdowns, but I scored a couple of times. We usually beat the other teams easily, except for the Jaycees, the south Bluefield team. Whenever we played the Jaycees, our coaches would harp on the fact that our players were disadvantaged compared to the rich kids in south Bluefield. Therefore, we needed to beat them at football to exact some form of revenge. That logic made absolutely no sense, but for elementary school players, I guess it provided some motivation.

After Pee Wee League for ages nine to ten, Midget League for ages eleven to twelve represented the next step up. When I moved to Midget League in the sixth grade, the coach moved me back to offensive guard. That season is another which has faded from my memory. I played sparingly since the seventh graders saw most of the playing time, and perhaps also because I was not playing in the position that turned out to be the best fit for me.

I played my last year of Midget football the same year I started junior high. Most seventh graders who still qualified as twelve-year-olds played in the Midget League. The Midget League expanded outside the city limits in 1970. Since I lived outside the city limits, I was zoned to play for one of the new teams in Bluewell. However, the league made an exception for Martin Jarrell and me, allowing us to continue playing with the American Legion, the team we had both played for in the past. After considering my options, I decided to go with the new team, knowing I would be more likely to play fullback for Bluewell, which would allow me to carry the ball rather than play on the offensive line. We faced the American Legion team in our first game, and we played to a 0–0 tie. As a new team to the league, we considered the outcome a moral victory.

As the season progressed, I became more comfortable running the ball. I remember after one of our games, the opposing coach found me and told me he looked forward to seeing me play in the future. That's when I started gaining confidence that one day in the not-so-distant future, perhaps I could play for the Beavers.

Chapter Three

New Experiences
Junior High, 1970–1973

I entered Central Junior High School in the fall of 1970. Central, formerly Beaver High School prior to the new Bluefield High being built in the 1950s, stood in the middle of a residential neighborhood. The four-story red brick building looked a bit like a high-walled fortified castle complete with two tower-like structures on either side of its front. The circular towers even had cut-out battlements at the top like one might see on a castle. It rose above all the other buildings and occupied an entire block on a steep hill overlooking the railway tracks which ran along the northern edge of Bluefield. Central had no playing fields or grass of any kind near the school. The gym and school offices were located on the main floor with three floors of classrooms above the main floor. Changing classrooms every period while keeping books and other belongings in a locker was a new experience for me. It took some time to get used to. Central was one of two junior highs in Bluefield for students in grades seven through nine. The other was Fairview Junior High in south Bluefield.

Each grade at Central was divided into several classes of about twenty students. Students were assigned to classes based on elementary school academic performance. The school placed the top academic students in class 7A before classes even started, unless they played in the band, in which case they were placed in 7B. The remaining students were assigned to 7C and so on through 7G. I was placed in 7A along with many of my good friends and continued to perform well academically in junior high, winning several year-end academic awards at the completion of each school year.

Gym class happened to be one of the few classes in which the 7A students interacted with students in other classes. Many of the kids with whom I had played American Legion football were in my gym class. My seventh-grade gym class shared the gym with a ninth-grade class. On various occasions, we played with or against the ninth graders. A game of dodge ball could turn ruthless. We divided into two teams, often seventh grade versus ninth grade, and positioned one team on each end of the basketball court. The gym teacher rolled three slightly deflated volleyballs out to half court and the game commenced. When a player got hit with a ball, he exited the game unless he managed to catch the ball. In that case, the player who threw the ball was out. This rule encouraged participants to throw the ball as hard as possible and, generally, high or low to minimize the chances of the ball being caught. An opponent's face and head were supposedly off-limits, but hitting someone in the face did not draw any penalty. Therefore, it was a fair target as far as we were concerned. The first team to lose all its players lost the game. The most interesting moments occurred when one team controlled all three balls. This forced the other team to line up with their backs literally against the wall waiting to see which player had been targeted for elimination. Generally, the three players with the balls would agree to target one kid so that he had little chance of dodging all three balls. Even if they missed, the ball would simply bounce off the cinder block wall directly back to the throwers. Despite the intensity, or perhaps because of it, dodgeball became my favorite game in gym class. I also think the game helped make all of us a little bit tougher.

Another unusual contest we played in gym was called crab-ball. The game resembled soccer except players crawled on their hands and feet with their backs to the floor. The idea was to kick an oversized inflated ball, about thirty inches in diameter, into the other team's wall. However, since crawling in an awkward position made it difficult to see, we ended up mostly crawling around the gym floor and kicking each other.

Other than gym, the only class I shared with kids outside my A group was my eighth-grade shop class. Girls attended home economics class while boys learned woodworking skills in shop. The teacher, who had one glass eye and limited vision, did not put up with any foolishness. He could not afford to let things get out of control given the fact his class consisted of thirteen-year-old boys with drills, band saws, and other tools. I say thirteen-year-old boys, but I think at least two of the guys in my class were closer to sixteen. They may have even driven themselves to school. Those guys did not care about shop class or any other class. They were simply passing time until they could legally drop out of school.

For our main academic classes, I enjoyed the company of essentially the same twenty students for three straight years. Teachers welcomed our class each day because we rarely gave them any problems. For the most part, we behaved as expected and focused on learning.

During this thirteen-to-fifteen age range, some of my classmates were starting to develop relationships with the opposite sex, but I continued to unsuccessfully pursue the object of my affection since first grade, Cathy.

Although some couples seemed to be constantly making out before and after school, I did not kiss a girl until my last month of junior high. That girl happened to be Cathy. Finally, it happened. However, to be fully transparent, I must say it happened for one reason only. While playing spin-the-bottle at an end-of-school party, I luckily landed the barrel of the bottle on Cathy. Well, perhaps not all luck, as I deliberately tried to time the speed of the rotation. Still, the kiss was optional in this game. The selected couple went into a separate room away from the rest of the group where they could kiss, shake hands, or do nothing. I considered it a victory.

Athletics

The seventh-grade basketball team was my first athletic team at Central. I made the twelve-player roster, but I rarely got the chance to play since our team included other more naturally gifted basketball players. I also earned a spot on the team in the eighth

28

grade, but again, I mainly sat on the bench. After that season, I wisely decided to give up basketball.

After playing my final year of Midget League football in the seventh grade, the time came to join the Central football team in the fall of 1971. Since our school did not have a practice field nearby, we suited up in our locker room and then rode a school bus to a field about two miles away for practice. I use the term locker room generously. It was essentially a dungeon-like room in the underground basement of our school, which makes sense for a school that resembled a castle.

The locker room stood adjacent to a coal storage bin and coal-powered furnace which served as the primary heat source for the school. The raw smell of coal mixed with sweaty football uniforms is not easily forgotten. The locker room had no windows and dreadfully dim lighting. I fully expected to encounter a rat every time I entered, but fortunately that never happened. Despite its shortcomings, the room served its purpose as a place to change clothes, put on equipment, and shower after a practice or game.

Our practice field fared just slightly better than the bleak condition of our locker room. It was surrounded on three sides by an expansive asphalt parking lot used for both Mitchell Stadium and Bowen Field, the city's baseball park on the opposite end. Our practice field was about the size of a football field, but that was not its original purpose. The carnival, which came to town each summer, set up its rides and amusements on that piece of land, consisting mostly of dirt and weeds. When we began practice in August, we had no idea what leftover debris from the carnival we would encounter. We usually practiced until around five o'clock during the school year. I always welcomed the sound of the bells of nearby Bluefield College signaling the end of practice had arrived.

Johnny Beckett, John Disibbio, and Carl Strong coached our junior high team. Coach Disibbio played on Bluefield's 1962 championship team and Coach Beckett played on the 1965 championship team. Coach Beckett was the older brother of Joey Beckett. Joey had attended a different elementary school, but he became one of my best friends throughout junior high and high school.

On our 1971 team, I was the second team fullback on offense and first team outside linebacker on defense. The first team fullback, Jaycee Collins, was an eighth grader like me, but the rest of the backfield consisted of ninth graders. Unlike Midget League, where we represented a team from a certain section of town, I felt a sense of pride representing my school. I loved that aspect of the game. For the first time, I boarded a school bus with my teammates and rode to games rather than hopping out of my parents' car at the stadium. This was also my first opportunity to face teams from nearby towns such as Beckley and Princeton. We had always viewed Princeton as one of our main rivals. However, Beckley consistently fielded better teams and had often been a thorn in Bluefield High School's schedule throughout the years. We finished the 1971 season with a 2–6 record, including two losses to Princeton and two losses to schools in Beckley. There was nothing special about that season and certainly nothing to indicate that brighter days may lie ahead.

In the spring of 1972, I participated for the first time in track and field. In elementary school, I always thought of myself as a fast runner, but apparently, I did not possess quite enough speed to compete in the sprint events for Central. No worries. We would need to field participants for numerous other events. On the bus ride back to school the day before our first track meet, I recall hearing the coaches discuss who would be entered into which events the following day. I overheard one coach say "Let's put Jackson in the mile run. At least he won't quit."

Now I do not recall ever running a mile in practice or at any other point in my life before that day. Football conditioning consisted of wind sprints. Nevertheless, the coaches had designated me as one of Central's participants in the mile run at the next day's track meet. In keeping with my underdog status and total lack of long-distance training, I finished in last place. I also finished in last place at the next meet and the next. Finally, I encountered the opportunity to beat at least one person when we held a dual meet against Fairview. Both schools agreed to let five people from each squad run the event rather than the usual limit of three. Being an experienced miler by this time, I knew I could beat at least one person to the finish line. It did not happen. I came in last place at every single track meet that spring. It came to the point my dad stopped asking me how I did. By that time, my confidence had suffered a severe hit. Without a doubt, I knew I needed to find another event for the next track and field season.

Ninth Grade

In the fall of 1972, the coaching staff decided to move me to left halfback, since the team needed a halfback and Jaycee was returning as the starting fullback. The decision to move me to halfback turned out to be the best thing that could have happened for me. It changed my football career from that point forward. The starting backfield for our junior high team consisted of Joey Beckett at quarterback, Jeff Simmons at right halfback, Jaycee Collins at fullback, and me at left halfback. We played our cross-town rival, Fairview, to a 6–6 tie in the season opener and later defeated them in our second meeting.

When we played Princeton in our fifth game of the season, I injured my left hand just below the base of my thumb. I finished the game, which we lost, but the pain in my hand continued. That evening, my mom took me to the emergency room for an x-ray. It turned out I had a small fracture of my hand, and the hospital's emergency staff put my entire hand in a plaster cast up to my elbow. I was extremely upset because I would miss the last three games of the season. I pleaded with my parents, claiming that my hand did not hurt that badly after all, and it had been a mistake to go to the emergency room. Finally, my mom agreed to take me to a well-known orthopedic surgeon in our area. Dr. Raub examined my hand and said he would remove the cast if Mom and I agreed. He offered to wrap my thumb with a metal splint surrounded by foam, and he thought the chances for further damage were slim. Besides, if I did damage it again, he said he could fix it. Without any hesitation, I asked him to remove the cast. The official rules of football allowed a player to participate in a game with foam padding but not with a plaster cast. I was thrilled to have the opportunity to finish the season. The coaches did not let me carry the ball the last three games. I played mainly on defense, but I finished the season with my teammates. That was important to me. We ended our season with a record of 3–4–1—only a slight improvement from our 2–6 record in 1971.

When spring track season rolled around, I made the decision I would do anything necessary to avoid the mile run. My friend Joey participated in both the low and high hurdles. Since I liked to hang out with him during practice, I decided to become a hurdler too. I quickly learned that hurdling entailed much more than simply running fast and jumping over obstacles in the way. The keys to success included taking the minimum number of steps between hurdles and clearing the hurdle quickly. The best hurdlers took three steps between hurdles, something all hurdlers did by high school, but most junior high boys took five steps. By taking three or five steps between hurdles, a runner could jump using the same leg—either right or left—to clear each hurdle. Since most junior high guys took five steps, they had to shorten or chop their last stride before each hurdle. Taking extra steps took extra time. I learned to clear hurdles with both my right and left legs, allowing me to take four steps between hurdles. With a little practice, it became quite natural for me to alternate between right and left on each hurdle.

By making this simple change, I became competitive in both the low and high hurdles. I finished in the top three in each event at several track meets that spring. Finishing in the top three, rather than finishing in last place, represented quite a change from the previous season. My confidence received a tremendous boost by the time I exited junior high. Running hurdles also increased my speed by forcing me to lengthen my stride. For any athlete, improving speed is a huge advantage.

The most memorable track meet of the 1973 spring season occurred at Greenbrier County. The weather turned quite cold for a day in May, with morning temperatures slightly above freezing. The asphalt track lacked any cushion. I caught my trailing foot on one of the high hurdles about halfway through a qualifying race that morning and fell forward. I broke my fall with my hands and ended up scraping both of my palms, both knees, and a shoulder. The coaches cleaned up the scrapes and bandaged my hands and knees as best they could. When the time rolled around for my next event, I showed up at the starting line still wrapped in white gauze and tape. The starter for the event was the head football coach of Greenbrier East High School, Coach Bob Zopp. He looked at me somewhat confused and asked me why I was running if I was injured. I told him I was running because I was scheduled to run. Coach Zopp asked for my name, and I told him. I didn't think anything else about it.

About three weeks later, after our track season ended, we held our year-end sports banquet in the Central Junior High cafeteria. The guest speaker that evening was Coach John Chmara, the head football coach of Bluefield High. I had never met Coach Chmara, but I knew a lot about him since I had religiously followed Beaver football for years. In less than three months, I would be trying to play football for Bluefield with him as my coach. It seemed surreal. Before dinner, our coaches introduced each of the rising sophomores to Coach Chmara. Of course, that was a big thrill for me, but the best part of the evening was yet to come. After dinner,

Coach Chmara delivered his speech. He talked at length about the importance of the pipeline to Bluefield High from Central and Fairview. He said he looked forward to seeing us in August and getting to know each of us. Then he ended his speech with this story: "I spoke with a colleague of mine the other day. He told me he had recently caught a small glimpse of why Bluefield enjoyed so much success on the football field. Coach Bob Zopp of Greenbrier East told me he had been assisting at a track meet a couple of weeks ago when one of the Central runners experienced a hard fall. He said many boys would have been done for the day. But not only did the Central boy get up, he showed up at the starting line ready to run again later that morning. That boy showed the determination and toughness it takes to be a winner."

My heart pounded in my chest. There I sat, listening to my future coach whom I had just met, convey a story making me the focal point. Then Coach Chmara said, "I want to thank Donnie Jackson for demonstrating those qualities to Coach Zopp." In hindsight, I understand Coach Chmara simply used the story to connect a current Central athlete to his speech. But that did not lessen the thrill. I could not wait to get home and tell my dad. It made for an exciting ending to my junior high days!

Chapter Four

High Hopes
Sophomore Year, 1973–1974

August 1, 1973. The first day of high school football practice. After placing my clothes into locker number 18, I put on my Bluefield Beavers number 18 maroon-and-white embossed shorts, t-shirt, and cleats for the first time. I stood in a genuine locker room—nothing like the Central Junior High dungeon locker room. From floor to ceiling, the entire room conveyed cleanliness with everything in its proper place. I would soon understand why the locker room stayed perpetually spotless as I learned more about Coach Chmara and his disciplined methods.

I had been assigned to locker 18 in late July upon completion of our physical exams for the upcoming season. After we completed our physicals, the coaches assigned lockers to the rising ninth graders. We could choose any vacant locker with the understanding the locker number would be our uniform number. For the most part, the available lockers were the ones vacated by the previous year's departing senior class. One of those seniors had been a running back who wore jersey number 17. I wore number 17 one season when I played Midget League football. I decided to take that number. However, I happened to be standing between lockers 17 and 18, talking to my friend, Joey, who had chosen number 19, when one of the assistant coaches, Coach Ferrell, came over to record our names and locker numbers.

He looked at me and said, "You're taking locker number 18, right?"

Without thinking, I said, "Yes sir," since I did not want to disagree with him right off the bat and make a bad first impression. I was already intimidated. No reason to make matters worse by trying to explain why I could not follow instructions and stand directly in front of the locker I originally wanted. From that moment on, I wore number 18.

When I arrived back at home that evening, I explained to Dad how I received my new jersey number. Dad said to me, "That's okay. There have been several good players at Bluefield who wore number 17. Perhaps you can make people remember number 18." He was joking of course, but at least he put a positive spin on my number assignment.

The West Virginia High School Athletic Association did not allow players to wear helmets or pads during the first week of practice. Therefore, we spent the majority of the first week working on physical conditioning, while learning the offensive playbook and defensive schemes. During the first few days of practice, I also learned the following inflexible rules of Bluefield High football.

Do not be late. Summer practices began at 8:27 a.m. with roll call in the back room—a separate small windowless room down the hallway from the main locker area. If we were not dressed and waiting in the back room before the coaches came in, we were late. If late, we were given what the coaches called a "six-thirty" for the next day. A "six-thirty" required a player to be at the school track at 6:30 the next morning to run laps. It constituted the primary form of punishment for virtually any violation of a myriad of team rules. Receiving a "six-thirty" created a logistical hardship for sophomores and their parents, since most sophomores could not yet drive.

Leave nothing outside our lockers while at practice or after practice. We were required to place all our belongings in our locker and lock it. Then, we hung the key to our locker's padlock in its assigned spot on the key rack. The metal folding chair assigned to the locker had to be folded and placed on top of the locker. If anything was not precisely where it should be, we were given a "six-thirty." That included leaving any articles of clothing outside the locker, leaving the key in the padlock, leaving a chair on the floor, etc.

Leave nothing on the shower room floor. The upper classmen tasked all sophomores with the job of making sure all soap bars were placed in their holders and not on the floor. Since the coaches could not possibly identify exactly who left soap on the floor, the one time it happened, the entire team enjoyed meeting at 6:30 the following morning. Problem solved.

Every question posed by a coach required an answer ending with "sir." This included any question before, during or after practice. Even the roll call had to be answered, "Here, sir." The coaches did not hand out a "six-thirty" if someone failed to address them as sir, but the glare in the coach's eye was all that was needed to remind them of this requirement.

Seniors were expected to lead. Sophomores did whatever any upperclassman told them to do. Seniors taught sophomores the rules.

Even though the rules may have seemed petty, they served a valid purpose. They were designed to instill discipline. Discipline comprised the foundation of Coach Chmara's program and Bluefield's success. He left no doubt about who was in charge and what he expected of us.

The first three weeks of practice consisted of two-a-days, meaning we practiced in the morning and afternoon with about a two-hour break for lunch. We brought our own lunches. Each day of August, for the next three years, I ate the same lunch—two sandwiches made of white bread, mayonnaise, salt, and the best tomatoes ever grown straight from my dad's garden, along with a half-gallon of sweet tea. The tomatoes usually started getting ripe around the end of July, just in time for football practices. It may not sound like much to eat, but I did not want to go into the afternoon practice feeling stuffed.

Guys ate their lunches in various spots, but my close friends and I always ate in the shade of the school building overlooking the parking lot and practice fields. This strategically located spot allowed us to watch the cheerleaders practice while we ate lunch. I did not know any of the cheerleaders when I was a sophomore, but that would change over the next two years as many of my friends joined the squad.

Practice sessions followed a standard pattern. We started practice with stretching exercises and calisthenics, followed by various position drills, then running through offensive and defensive plays as a team, and finally ending with conditioning. The conditioning drill we dreaded the most after practice was known as running a *suribachi*. Named after the mountain on Iwo Jima made famous in a World War II photo, a *suribachi* consisted of running up and down a hill at the south end of the practice field ... essentially the base of East River Mountain. We usually started out with about ten the first day and then worked our way up from there. The coaches rewarded us for what they deemed good practices with fewer *suribachis* or with wind sprints. Running sprints always came as a welcome break.

After a week of practice in shorts and another week in shorts and helmets, we eagerly looked forward to practicing in full pads, starting August 15th. Practicing in full pads meant we could finally block and tackle—real football! However, no one looked forward to the numerous hitting drills that could now be done in full pads. During the first morning of practice in pads, we did nothing but drills. Finally, as the morning session came to an end, Coach Chmara told us it was time to scrimmage. With much excitement, our first team offense lined up against our first team defense. The offense ran one play which took all of fifteen to twenty seconds. Then, Coach Chmara said, "That's enough. Everyone to the hill." So, we went to the hill to run *suribachis,* carrying the extra weight of our pads.

As a sophomore, I tried to volunteer for the practice squad, or "scout team" as it was called, every chance I got. The scout team served as the opposition for our first and second units in practice. Our 1973 team was loaded with seniors, many of whom had played important roles as juniors on the 1972 team—the team that had gone undefeated in the regular season prior to losing a 34–32 double-overtime heartbreaker to Dupont High in the state semi-finals at Laidley Field in Charleston. The chances of a sophomore competing for a starting position were slim. Accordingly, I made it my goal to simply work my way up the depth chart and put myself in position to get into a game whenever the opportunity arose—meaning whenever we had a big lead. Having made the playoffs the previous year, we entered the 1973 season with high expectations that this team would return to the playoffs and possibly deliver Bluefield its first AAA state championship since 1967.

I started preseason practices as the fourth team left halfback behind a returning senior and two juniors. Yes ... fourth team. One of the juniors left the team in early August and I moved up to third team. Not bad, I thought. Making progress. Then, something totally unexpected happened. After the first week of practice in pads, Coach Chmara told Jaycee Collins and me to join the linemen for drills. As we jogged over to join the linemen, my mind was spinning. I felt like saying, "This is a mistake! Eighteen is not even a lineman's number." The fact he sent Jaycee with me, rather than me alone, is the only thing that made it somewhat bearable. I started practicing at left end.

I tried to convince myself that playing left end might not be entirely bad. I could catch passes and run with the ball after the catch. Who was I kidding? I took some comfort in the fact I had not been moved to offensive guard like I had been in PeeWee and Midget leagues. But no matter how hard I tried, I never sold myself on the switch.

Practicing with the linemen was tough. Coach Ferrell and Coach Linkous loved to see the linemen hitting blocking sleds … and each other. I accepted this move solely as part of Coach Chmara's plan to develop Jaycee and me into more physical players, but he never once told me that. I think I became a better blocker and more accustomed to contact, but I can't say that with certainty. At the end of practice, the linemen were often required to participate in what we called a "board drill." The backs were dismissed after conditioning to go to the locker room while the linemen went to the boards. As I watched the running backs jog off the practice field while I remained, I kept asking myself, "What did I do to deserve this?"

The boards were literally two-inch-by-six-inch hardwood boards about eight feet long. Two players straddled the board on each end, facing one another in a four-point stance. On the command, "Hit!", each player tried to drive the other player backwards off the end of the board. The winner earned the right to be released to the locker room. The loser stayed for another round. In case of a tie, both players stayed unless Coach Ferrell deemed the effort sufficient to release both players. We would make loud noises, grunts, and groans in our attempt to demonstrate sufficient effort.

Coach Chmara and Johnny Beckett, my coach at Central who had moved up to the high school coaching ranks, coached the backs and the offense. Tom Ferrell and Chuck Lambert coached the linemen and the defense. I had known Coach Lambert for several years. He lived in my Harry Heights neighborhood for a short period of time, and his son attended elementary school with me. He possessed a jovial and somewhat light-hearted demeanor. Coach Ferrell, conversely, stood firmly on the other end of the spectrum. He functioned as the intimidator, the enforcer, the in-your-face motivator that all teams need. He also supervised the six-thirty disciplinary workouts. All our coaches continually assessed the younger players with the intention of grooming us for the future.

School Starts

Thankfully, the start of classes signaled the end of two-a-day practices. I looked forward to meeting my teachers and my new classmates from Fairview Junior High. Of course, I had already met the football players from Fairview, but I was thinking more about meeting the dozens of new girls. It seemed like an appropriate time to start scouting for a potential new girlfriend since my long-time affection for the girl I had pursued since first grade was never reciprocated. Nine years was enough. Time to move on. I did not plan to start dating before getting my driver's license. Since I did not turn sixteen until March, I had plenty of time to make new friendships without putting any pressure on myself to ask someone on a date.

Our first game on September 7, 1973, pitted us against our traditional cross-town rival, Graham High School. Graham's head coach, Glen Carlock, had been an assistant coach for both Coach Gainer and Coach Chmara prior to accepting the Graham position. From the stories I heard about him, he acted as the enforcer whose role now fell to Coach Ferrell.

During the Thursday practice prior to each game, the coaches made their final decisions as to which players would get to suit up, or dress out as we called it, for the following night's game. After a light practice, the starters and key reserves on offense and defense returned to the locker room. This group generally consisted of about twenty players who by necessity were required to be in uniform on Friday. The remaining thirty players, including all sophomores, then scrimmaged for about forty-five minutes in a tradition known as pride practice. At the end of pride practice, the assistant coaches took turns choosing players who would be allowed to suit up with the team until a designated limit was reached. The players not chosen to suit up were given a ticket to sit in the stands on Friday night. The entire process created nervous energy among all of us. One mistake or fumble could easily cost a player the opportunity to dress out. No one wanted to practice all week and then sit in the stands with the other students. Fortunately, I was chosen to dress out for the first game and all subsequent games. A couple of times the coaches selected me late in the draft, but I think they intentionally built up the drama to ensure we did not get complacent and take suiting up for granted. Some of my sophomore friends did not get to dress for all our games. However, this problem did not exist the following year as I will explain later.

Opening Night

The Friday of my first game as a Bluefield Beaver is ingrained in my memory. I participated for the first time in a routine which I would come to know well over the next three years. On Friday morning in the locker room before school, we took a test about our opponent and the game plan for that evening. If we did not do well on the test, the threat of being removed from the dress squad loomed over us. I do not recall anyone ever failing the test. We spent so much time in practices during the week going over our detailed game plan, the test served merely as a formality.

On game days, the players wore team-issued maroon blazers with "We Believe" stitched in white above the front left pocket, matching the motto also displayed on the side of our helmets. I beamed with pride as I walked the hallways that day. I had trouble staying focused in my classes. My mind kept leaping ahead to the end of the school day. All I could think about was finally getting the chance to put on a Bluefield game jersey and run out of the locker room in front of the ten thousand fans in attendance. And yes, ten thousand people typically came to Bluefield High School football games. When school finally ended, the players gathered in the locker room and relaxed for a couple of hours until about 5:00 p.m. Then, the coaches told us we could go to the cafeteria for dinner.

The pre-game meal which we consumed that night remained the same for the next three years: roast beef, mashed potatoes, carrots, peas, and a roll. After dinner, we gathered in the school gym for the coaches to go over one last walk-through of who would be on the field for offense, punting, defense, punt return, kickoff, kick return, onside kick return, etc. The coaches then gave us any last-minute instructions or reminders about that night's opponent. After they finished, we hurried back to the locker room to put on our uniforms, and then we waited in the back room until the coaches told us to board the bus.

We owned our own school bus, painted maroon and white, for transporting the coaches and players from the high school to Mitchell Stadium, about three miles away for home games. As we approached, the crowds making their way into the stadium created a narrow path for our bus through the parking lot and up a small ramp leading to the home locker room. Looking out my window, I was in awe of the many fans waving and admiring us in an almost reverential manner. The coaches demanded total silence on the ride to the stadium. We exited the bus to make our way into the locker room in single file. Once inside the stadium's stone-covered locker room, we waited about ten minutes before going out on the field for warm up exercises. Pre-game and warm up exercises lasted about twenty-five minutes until 7:45 p.m. We then returned to the locker room while the band performed the National Anthem. During the few minutes leading up to kickoff, the coaches did not say much. By this time, there was not much left to be said. Although religion was not a focal point in any way, shape, or form, we always said the Lord's Prayer right before exiting our locker room to roaring cheers and ovations from our fans for the 8:00 p.m. kick off. We exited in single file before sprinting to our bench, accompanied by the sound and words of our fight song: "Maroon and white, we'll win tonight!" And we always believed we would win.

We defeated Graham handily that night for the tenth straight season by a final score of 36–12. Late in the game, the assistant coaches prepared a lineup to replace the starters, and Coach Lambert called on me to play left end. This came as a surprise because I still considered myself a running back even though the 1973 football program listed me as a running back/end. I tried to look past the fact my position photo in the football program was included with the ends; Freddy Simon, Jerry Neal, David Litz, Brian Bruckner, Randy Albert, and me. Since I did not enter the game as a running back with the second team, I concluded I must have been on the third team opening night depth chart. I certainly did not consider myself the second team left end, but the usual second team left end had already played most of the night on defense, so I got my chance to get into the game. We ran only three or four plays until time expired, but the number of plays was irrelevant. I had now officially played for the Bluefield Beavers!

Weekend Routine

The following morning, I learned even more about the routine of playing football at Bluefield. The coaches required us to report to the school locker room on Saturday morning after each game to get treatment for injuries, go through a light workout, and most importantly, clean and polish our game helmets and game cleats. We used different helmets and cleats for games than we did for practice. That first post-game Saturday morning, I learned about the requirement to totally clean and wax our helmets. Any paint marks or scratches we might have received from an opponent's helmet the night before had to be removed. Our cleats also had to be cleaned and polished with black polish on the shoe and white polish on the trim. This sounded easy enough, especially since I had been on the field for only a handful of plays and my equipment remained almost spotless. I waxed my helmet, polished my cleats, and returned them to the equipment room.

However, no one could return their gear and leave for the day until Coach Ferrell inspected their helmet and shoes. Taking out his pocketknife, he scratched into the groove between the shoe and the sole until he found a miniscule piece of dirt. Citing my inadequate cleaning performance, he told me to clean and polish my cleats again. When I returned them, he took out his knife and searched the bottom of my cleats for flakes of white paint from the Mitchell Stadium field striping. He then told me to clean and polish them again. The struggle to get my helmet and cleats accepted by Coach Ferrell constituted part of the sophomore hazing ritual. Juniors and seniors passed inspection more easily, in part because experience had taught them all possible locations where paint or dirt could hide in a football cleat.

On Sunday afternoons, we again returned to the school to watch film of Friday night's game in the back room. Yes, playing Bluefield football required you to be at the high school every single day of the week from the first game of the season until the season ended. I quickly learned that watching game film with coaches was nothing at all like watching a football game on television. Our video team recorded our games on 16mm film, and the coaches probably watched the film at least three times before we arrived on

Sunday.

We watched each play at least four or five times while the coaches offered up constructive criticism—and occasional praise——for each player's performance. Given all the flaws the coaching staff found, it was miracle we could beat anyone. Without question, I credit those Sunday afternoon film sessions as one of the primary reasons for our success over the years. By pointing out to each player what he had done correctly or incorrectly, each of us were made aware that we had plenty of room for improvement. Film review served as a great teaching tool.

Coach Chmara often emphasized, "Every play is designed to score a touchdown if it is executed perfectly." The film sessions allowed us to see what he meant by that statement.

Back to the Season

We faced our cross-county rival, Princeton High School, in our second game of the season. Like Graham, we had beaten them for several consecutive years. This season turned out to be no exception. We considered our rivalry with Princeton at least as intense, if not more so, than our rivalry with Graham. Our game with Princeton generally carried more weight under the West Virginia playoff system since Graham played in a smaller classification in Virginia. The Princeton game represented my first game on the road. For away games, we normally rode an air-conditioned motor coach, but since this trip lasted no more than twenty minutes, we rode our maroon-and-white school bus.

We defeated Princeton 50–8, and I again got the opportunity

to play in the game. More importantly, after a few offensive plays at left end, the coaches allowed me to move to halfback for a couple of plays. I carried the ball one time that night for a gain of three yards—not exactly an overwhelming debut but still my debut as a Beaver running-back. After two straight appearances, I started to think I might play in all our games that year, especially if we kept winning by these large margins!

But the streak ended the following week when I did not see any action in a 24–0 home win over Oak Hill. Coach Chmara refused to play any sophomores during the game due to his displeasure over pride practice the previous evening. Pride practice usually lasted less than twenty-five minutes. However, on that Thursday, we scrimmaged for about sixty minutes. When we arrived at school Friday morning for our weekly test, Coach Chmara told us some parents had complained to him about the length of Thursday's practice. His message to us: "You are welcome to leave the team if you or your parents are unhappy, but I do not want to hear from your parents ever again about any aspect of football practice." I knew he was not addressing me because my parents did not come to practices and had never spoken to Coach Chmara. I never learned which parents complained, but no one left the team and it never happened again. Since I did not play in the Oak Hill game, my primary goal for the evening consisted of trying to avoid stepping on any painted lines to reduce the time required to clean my cleats the following morning.

We traveled into the coalfields of McDowell County for our fourth game at Gary High School. By halftime, we had put the game out of reach. With a large lead, the second half presented the younger players an opportunity to get some playing time. Once again, I played a couple of series at left end before being moved to left halfback. I gained five yards on my single rushing attempt of the night, but that was almost double the output of my previous rushing yardage against Princeton. We won the game by a score of 54–0. During film review on Sunday, my blocking technique at left end became the subject of much ridicule. In the back of my mind, I kept thinking, *"Hey, I didn't sign up for offensive line in the first place."*

Coach Lambert said to me, "You look like an antelope out there trying to block."

Now, I am not exactly sure how an antelope would look on a football field, but I knew he did not intend it as a compliment. From that day on, my teammates occasionally chided me and called me "Antelope" for a laugh. On the flip side, I received much more encouraging comments from the coaches about my play at halfback. The following week, Coach Chmara no longer required Jaycee and me to practice with the linemen, and I never played tight end again.

The following week at Welch, we won easily by the score of 36–0. I carried the ball two times for fourteen yards, my first double-digit-yardage rushing game as a Beaver. I now proudly boasted four carries for twenty-two total yards on the season. Not a bad rushing average. The coaches seemed to be acknowledging and gaining more confidence in my running ability, but I never knew exactly where I stood with them that entire season.

Five games into the season, we sported a 5–0 record, and I had played in four of the five games. I felt certain I would contribute to the team over the second half of the regular season. At this point, I no longer worried about making the dress list at pride practice. I finally felt like I had earned my place on the team.

In week six, we hosted Woodrow Wilson of Beckley, one of our most difficult games every season. With an undefeated record, we were ranked fifth in the state and had outscored our opponents by a combined score of 200–20. Beckley came into the contest with a 4–1 record and ranked eighth. On the Friday morning of the game, we learned our starting quarterback, John Baker, was sick with the flu and could not play that night. With our starting quarterback sidelined, our offense seemed out-of-sync throughout the game. I question whether having our starting quarterback available would have made any difference. Beckley was one of the best teams in the state. They handed us an unexpected 20–6 loss. The star of the game for Beckley was a sophomore running back named Mike Lewis whom we would face twice more during my high school career. While Beckley featured a sophomore, none of our sophomores saw any action in the game.

The highlight game of my 1973 season came the following week at home against Greenbrier East, Coach Zopp's team, as fate would have it. On October 19, 1973, I carried the ball six times in a 57–0 win and scored my first touchdown for Bluefield High— something I had dreamed of since childhood. The following morning, I could not have been any happier reading the Bluefield Daily Telegraph, "Beaver's final touchdown was scored by Donnie Jackson on a seven-yard burst up the middle." That morning, I would have found it difficult to believe I had seen my final game action as a sophomore.

We had an open date on our schedule the next week. The coaches took advantage of this break by increasing our live scrimmages in practice. On Thursday, we played a scrimmage game matching the seniors against the juniors and sophomores. Almost all our starters on both offense and defense were seniors, so the matchup essentially came down to first team versus second team. I could call it a breakout game, or practice, for me. I managed to break a few tackles and get free for a couple of long gains against the senior defense. The seniors acted a little surprised that I had been able to run effectively against them, but they also expressed their compliments to me after practice. I fully respected Freddie Simon, Jerry Neal, Anthony Disibbio, Jim Kiser, Jim Brooks, David Thompson, David Lilly, and the other seniors on that team. Gaining their respect in turn was important to me. I certainly thought I would be able to contribute to the team during our last three games.

A Rough Ending

We hit the road again for our eighth game at third-ranked East Bank High School in the Charleston area. East Bank fielded an outstanding team with an all-state running back named Claude Geiger. We could not afford another loss, as two losses would certainly keep us out of the playoffs. Our seniors played with intensity and the game was tightly contested throughout. I believe we outplayed East Bank everywhere except on the scoreboard in a 20–6 loss. I did not get into the game since we needed our starters for the entire contest. East Bank proceeded to win the 1973 AAA state championship. We had lost to ultimately the best team in the state but did not know it at the time. The bus ride home from Charleston felt unusually long.

With our hopes of making the playoffs gone, our motivation waned. For a team that seemed destined to return to the playoffs, it was a hard pill to swallow. In week nine, we faced Northfork High, a smaller AA school from McDowell County, in our last home game of the season. Due to the hangover from our East Bank loss, we uncharacteristically did not play with our usual intensity and execution. Northfork had built its reputation as a basketball powerhouse. Bluefield normally did not schedule them in football, but they were added to fill a void in our schedule. However, in 1973, their football team was contending for a playoff spot. On that night, Northfork displayed more motivation, played harder, and ultimately won the game 22–18. They eventually won the 1973 AA state championship. I can say we underestimated them, but they earned the win. Again, I spent the night on the bench.

We closed out the 1973 season at Andrew Lewis High School in Roanoke, Virginia, on a windy night with freezing temperatures. I recall little about the game itself, primarily because I spent the entire game bundled up in my parka trying to keep warm. Football cleats and thin socks provided little warmth and my toes felt numb. I bounced up and down and ran in place on the sideline to prevent what I believed to be imminent frostbite. Despite the weather conditions, Andrew Lewis managed to kick a forty-seven-yard field goal on the last play of the game for a 23–20 win.

A season which began with the promise of a likely return to the state playoffs ended in disappointment. If not for a double overtime loss in 1972, the seniors on our team would have played for the state championship the previous fall. Now, due to some unfortunate twists, they ended their senior year with a 6–4 record, the worst record of any Bluefield team in recent memory. The results of that season drove home the lesson—do not take anything for granted. Meeting high expectations required both hard work and a bit of good fortune. That valuable lesson stuck with us as sophomores and eventually paid off.

Winter Workouts

The high school football days of the seniors on our team were over, but the returning sophomores and juniors faced several months of hard work to prepare for the next season. Upon returning to school from Thanksgiving weekend, we began that task. After school, we reported daily to the locker room for weight training and conditioning. I quickly learned weight training days were like vacation days compared to conditioning days. The coaches split us up into two groups at the start of winter workouts. One group lifted weights while the other group went to the back room for agility training. We alternated every other day.

On weight training days, we took turns rotating around the stations of a universal gym machine. If you were waiting on your turn at a station, you jumped rope while waiting. Usually, Coach Chmara worked in his office and kept an eye on us through his glass window. He would occasionally come out and walk around a little and then go back into his office. His style of supervising weight training matched his style of coaching football. Coach

Chmara always operated in a business-like manner. He did not try to become friends with his players. He was content being their coach.

We experienced a totally opposite reality in the back room. Coach Ferrell supervised the training and made it as excruciating as he could. A wrestling mat covered almost the entire floor of the approximately twenty-foot-by-twenty-foot, windowless room. Coach Ferrell always turned the heat as high as it would go. He must have done this around noon as the room felt like an oven by two-thirty, when conditioning began. The sessions lasted forty minutes but felt like two hours. We engaged in practically every conditioning drill imaginable for a room that size: up-downs, monkey rolls, circular sprints, wrestling, etc. The off-season conditioning program certainly played a major role in building Bluefield's football success. However, I could not wait for it to end on March 1; the day track season began.

Spring of '74

My sophomore track season proved to be uneventful. I participated in the high hurdles, low hurdles, and shuttle hurdle relay. Our best hurdler, my friend Joey, placed in the top three at several track meets. However, I do not remember much about the season other than going to the state track meet as part of the shuttle hurdle relay team.

That is not to say the spring of 1974 is lost from my memory. I fully remember turning sixteen and getting my driver's license. With this coming-of-age document now in hand, I prepared to go on my first real date. My parents purchased a used Dodge Demon with a butterscotch exterior and black interior for me to drive. The Dodge Demon did not go down in automotive history as a classic, but it served its purpose of getting me where I needed to go for the next few years. I had waited the better part of my sophomore year to earn the right to drive my own car on my first date. Now came the hard part— asking a girl to go out with me. The choice for me was easy. I spent many days of my sophomore year flirting in the hallways with Harriet Edwards, the daughter of a prominent local obstetrician and one of the nicest girls in our school. Harriet was one of the Fairview Junior High girls I had been eager to meet at the start of the school year. I asked Harriet to go see a movie, *The Sting*, starring Robert Redford and Paul Newman. I found it difficult to concentrate on the plot while I debated in my mind whether I should try to hold her hand. I think I finally got the courage to do so right before the film credits started rolling. My parents would have been fine if I'd asked her to marry me after our first date. However, that is not the way things work when you are sixteen years old. After a few dates, I decided I was not ready to be in a serious relationship. Going out with Harriet seemed like hitting a home run on my first swing. She eventually became one of our cheerleaders and our homecoming queen. Fortunately for me, I ended up with my own cheerleader and homecoming queen a few years later.

Summer Job

I got a job in the summer of 1974 with the City of Bluefield

58

Parks Department. The Parks Department had a pipeline with the football team. Along with about a dozen other football players, I picked up trash at the city park, cut weeds, and lined the softball fields.

On some days, the city staff assigned us to supervise children's playgrounds in other parts of the city. If the job sounds easy, that's because it was. We basically made four hours of work last for eight hours.

That summer I became good friends with David Litz, a rising senior and one of the football team's three returning starters. David possessed the greatest sense of humor and could imitate Coach Chmara's mannerisms and voice almost perfectly. He would shift into Coach Chmara mode at any given moment, and we all would crack up laughing. His humor provided great relief when things got tough. I had no idea at the time just how badly we would need his humor in the grueling days to come.

The summer flew by, and before I knew it, August rolled around again.

Chapter Five

Rebuilding
Junior Year, 1974–1975

With so many departed seniors filling starting roles in 1973, we opened practice in 1974 with nineteen of the twenty-two offensive and defensive positions up for grabs. Two starters returned on offense—John Baker at quarterback and David Litz at end. We returned one starter on defense—Charles Thomas at defensive back. I knew I would be in competition for the starting left halfback position with at least two other players, including a returning senior who alternated with me in 1973 as a back-up.

About sixty players showed up for the first day of practice. Coach Lambert had recently retired from coaching football, leaving us with only three coaches for the 1974 season. Our coaches were eager to put the disappointment of the prior season behind us. To do that, they needed to prepare our totally inexperienced team for the upcoming season. The coaching staff knew the talent level of the team when practice started in 1973.

Accordingly, preseason practices in 1973 may have been somewhat less strenuous. That was not the case on August 1, 1974. The coaches did not know who they could depend upon since most of us possessed no significant game experience. They decided to learn about our squad by making the preseason practices particularly hard.

On the first day of practice, Coach Chmara informed us about a change in our conditioning training. He told us, "We will no longer run *surabachis* (hills) at the end of practice."

The first thing that popped into my head—*fantastic!* We all hated running *surabachis,* and Coach Chmara must have finally realized that.

He then proceeded to explain. "Practice will be divided into four quarters, like a game. We will run *surabachi*s at the end of each quarter."

My second thought—*That's not too bad.* We can run four or five *surabachis* at the end of each quarter rather than running twenty at the end of practice. I had misinterpreted his remarks. Coach Chmara's idea consisted of running twenty at the end of each quarter. And we did this eight times per day during two-a-day practices! I believe we spent more time running up and down the hill than we did practicing football that August.

If Coach Chmara was looking to get rid of players who were not fully committed, then he succeeded. Each morning of practice that August, the ranks grew thinner. One morning, my main competitor for the left halfback position did not show up. He came back to practice the next day, but I guess the coaches did not like the reason he gave for missing the prior day, so they demoted him.

After that day, he never returned. In addition, the most experienced player of our three returning starters, our quarterback, decided to hang up his cleats that same day. Over a three-week period, we lost almost half the guys who showed up for our first practice. We ended the preseason with thirty-three players on our roster, including just four seniors. Our team was numerically thin, physically small, and young, but we were in great shape due to our conditioning work!

Our 1974 starting backfield consisted of Joey Beckett at quarterback, Jaycee Collins at fullback, Charles Thomas, one of our four seniors, at right halfback, and me at left halfback. I also earned a starting position at defensive back and a position on all special teams—kickoff, kick return, punting, and punt return. I would have no shortage of playing time this year. I was scheduled to stay on the playing field the entire game. Thursday pride practices ceased. Every player who survived preseason practices had earned the right to dress for games. I looked forward to finally playing a larger role in Bluefield High football, but to be honest, an enormous sense of uncertainty hung over all of us. With a roster full of experienced players the previous season, we had underperformed by Bluefield's standards. Would we do even worse this year? We had no idea how the season would unfold.

A New Season Begins

We faced an unfamiliar opponent on our schedule for our first game of the season, Stonewall Jackson High School of Charleston. Bluefield had not faced Stonewall Jackson since the 1967 state championship game. We opened the season at Mitchell Stadium on August 30, 1974. Stonewall Jackson featured a junior running back named Walter Easley, who scored two touchdowns as Stonewall Jackson handed us a 26–0 defeat. At halftime, we trailed 6–0, but we turned the ball over repeatedly in the second half to squander any possible chance of pulling off an upset. During a kickoff return late in the game, I tried to block one of the players on their kicking team by throwing my body into his legs. Not only did I draw a penalty flag for an illegal block below the waist, I also managed to hurt my left hand in the process. After examining my hand, our team physician decided I should not return to the game. X-rays after the game revealed a fracture of the metacarpal bone below my left index finger.

The injury turned out to be quite similar to the type of fracture I'd experienced two years earlier during my ninth-grade year at Central. I had invested too much time and effort to allow a minor fracture to derail my first season as a starter. Putting a cast on my hand was out of the question. Our team physician taped two metal splints on either side of the fractured bone and taped foam padding around the splints.

Watching game film on Sunday, Coach Chmara commented, "That's great. You broke your hand and drew a penalty on the same play." I lost my starting job at running back since the coaches did not want to risk letting me carry the ball with only one good hand. Fortunately, I kept my starting job on defense.

The following Friday on a rain-soaked Mitchell Stadium field, Graham defeated us 13–0, thereby ending their ten-year losing streak to Bluefield. Our team remained scoreless after two games.

I had no idea when, or if, I could regain my starting position at running back. Our season, and my role in it, could not have gotten off to a worse start. I struggled to cope with the fact our team was nothing like the Beaver teams I had grown up watching. Those teams rarely lost, and they certainly did not post zeroes on the Bluefield side of the scoreboard. My hopes of playing even a minor part on a winning team were evaporating before my eyes.

On Saturday morning, we cleaned our cleats and helmets as usual. David Litz invited me to attend a Boy Scout meeting with him later that morning. The Scout leaders thought it would be nice to have a couple of Beaver football players speak to the kids. We told Coach Ferrell, "We need to leave soon to go speak at a Boy Scout meeting."

"Why is that?" he asked.

"The den mothers want us to talk to the scouts about playing football."

"I hope you're not going to talk to them about how to tackle."

Ouch!

We faced Princeton at home on September 13, 1974. I was slated to start on defense once again, but Coach Chmara told me prior to the game he planned to work me back into the offense. Our struggling offense needed all the help it could get. Bluefield had not lost to Princeton since 1957. However, Princeton entered the game as a three-touchdown favorite. Princeton fans finally saw an opportunity to break the winless streak against Bluefield teams coached by Gainer and Chmara. Princeton scored first on a long run, but we responded with my second career touchdown, a thirty-one-yard run on a misdirection play called 26 Reverse. This specific play came to be one of my favorite plays throughout high school. I knew our two pulling guards, Rocky Malamisura and Joe Hager, would create a running lane. We went to halftime with the score tied 6–6.

Princeton scored to start the third quarter. We responded once again with my second touchdown of the night with 26 Reverse. The score remained deadlocked at 14–14 as Princeton drove for a potential go-ahead score late in the game. We stopped their drive at our four-yard line when I came up with my first high school interception. I returned the interception to the Princeton forty-one-yard line, but an illegal block wiped out most of the return yardage. With only seconds remaining, we had little chance of winning in regulation, but we had forced the game into overtime. However, I would not play a part in the overtime period because I had experienced leg cramps on the interception return and did not have enough time to alleviate them before the extra period began.

In overtime, each team received one possession starting at the ten-yard line. Princeton scored a touchdown on the second play of its possession and added the two-point conversion. We failed to respond on our possession, and Princeton held on for a 22–14 victory. Even though we lost, our offense showed signs of life. My hidden doubts about my role with the team started to subside. For the first time as a Beaver, and in my thirteenth game, I could finally say I had contributed in a meaningful way. After that night, I knew I would never worry again about whether I would start.

Leg cramps turned out to be a recurring problem for me because we did not know the importance of staying hydrated. We took salt tablets before games to supposedly help prevent cramping, but that may have made the problem worse. Leg cramps caused a sharp pain in my calf muscles, but they usually went away after a minute or two. They never stopped me in a crucial situation except for the Princeton game.

Despite our grueling preseason preparation, our record stood at 0–3, with all three games played at home. Counting the three losses at the end of last season, we had now lost six games in a row. The six losses equaled the total number of Bluefield losses from 1959 to 1968. Coach Chmara refused to make excuses. He simply told us we must get better, and we must learn how to win. He said we could easily fall into the habit of losing if we allowed it. He inspired us with his belief and confidence. We had started the season young and inexperienced, but we now had three games under our belt. As it turned out, Stonewall Jackson, our first opponent and first loss that year, would go on to win the 1974 AAA state championship. Years later, the Charleston Gazette newspaper called the 1974 Stonewall Jackson team the best team of all time in West Virginia. Graham ultimately won the '74 area championship, and Princeton posted its best season since the 1950s. We deserved to be underdogs in our first three games. We had lost to three good teams.

Learning to Win

We played our first road game of the season the following Friday at Oak Hill. Due to a penalty, my only touchdown of the game was called back in the first half as we played to a 0–0 halftime score. However, I rushed for over a hundred yards and three different teammates scored touchdowns in the second half as we earned our first win of the season 20–15. We played with the intensity Coach Chmara had been seeking. Our defense stopped Oak Hill on a late drive to preserve the victory and end Bluefield's six-game losing streak.

Back at home the following week, we easily defeated Gary 39–6. I scored three touchdowns in the first half of the game and now totaled five touchdowns in five games. With five touchdowns and two two-point conversions, I appeared on the list of area scoring leaders for the first time. During the season, the Bluefield Daily Telegraph published a weekly list of scoring leaders at area high schools. Our area included a couple dozen schools in both West Virginia and Virginia. After being shut out our first two games, I considered it an honor to represent our team at the halfway point of the season.

On October 4, 1974, we faced Welch at home. Coach Chmara missed the entire week of practice leading up to the game due to the death of his brother in Pittsburgh. Coach Beckett and Coach Ferrell prepared us for the game that week. In the first half, both teams kept trading scores. Welch scored three times and we answered with a touchdown of our own each time. We kicked one extra point and stopped Welch on all three of its extra point attempts for a 19–18 lead at halftime. In the second half, our defense stepped up with two goal line stands after our offense turned the ball over deep in our own territory. That game brought us together as a team and showed us we could do whatever it took to win. We came through with clutch plays at the right moments in a game we could have easily lost. Different people stepped up to make key plays. Neither team scored in the second half. We won 19–18 and evened our record at 3–3.

Another Tough Test

We faced a formidable opponent in our next game on the road at Beckley against the undefeated Flying Eagles. This game held little promise for us to get back above breakeven on the season. My left hand was almost completely healed, so I removed the metal splints and played with just a small foam pad covering my hand. We trailed 14–0 at halftime and lost 38–14. I scored on a seventy-five-yard touchdown run in the second half and ended the game with more rushing yards than Mike Lewis, Beckley's junior all-state running back. Unfortunately, those yards did not translate into points. Beckley finished the 1974 season undefeated. However, they missed the playoffs after finishing fifth in the final regular season rankings. In my opinion, Beckley and Stonewall Jackson were the two best teams in West Virginia in 1974. The points-based playoff system did not allow them to play each other since Beckley did not qualify as one of the top four teams. A weak schedule hurt Beckley that year.

Finishing Strong

We traveled to Greenbrier East the following Friday again as underdogs. Greenbrier East came into the game with a 5–1 record compared to our 3–4 record. Our schedule in 1974 had not been easy. Of the four teams that had beaten us, three remained undefeated, and the other, Princeton, had lost just once. The one loss on Greenbrier East's record came at the hands of undefeated Beckley. On Greenbrier East's first play of the game, I recovered a fumble and returned it fifty-seven yards for a touchdown. Unfazed, Greenbrier East scored the next two touchdowns as the game swung back and forth. The game felt like the Princeton game or the Welch game where both teams appeared to be evenly matched. Late in the fourth quarter, we trailed 35–27 and needed a touchdown plus a two-point conversion to tie the game. We faced a third and long situation on our crucial last drive when Coach Chmara called our final timeout. Thinking that Greenbrier East expected a pass, he instead called a running play designed for me to carry the ball right up the middle of the field. During the timeout, he called me over to the sideline and told me, "Try to get out of bounds to stop the clock if you can." *How am I supposed to get out of bounds on a play called up the middle?* That was my thought, but I certainly didn't ask Coach Chmara that question. I determined to try and do what he asked of me, unlikely as it might seem, because I always tried to do whatever he asked. I broke through the line of scrimmage and headed for the sideline, picking up the first down and getting out of bounds.

Moments later, Joey scored a touchdown on a short run, and we then added the critical two points needed to tie the game at 35–35. In overtime, Greenbrier East got the ball first and scored a touchdown but failed on their two-point conversion attempt. That left the door open for us to win. I carried the ball to the five-yard-line. Charles Thomas added a yard to the four, and on third down, I carried the ball into the end zone to tie the game. Brian Bruckner kicked the extra point and we walked off the field 42–41 winners.

With nine touchdowns on the season, I now stood in third place on the list of area scoring leaders, but I was equally proud of the role I played on our defense. Our team had, in fact, come together. We understood each other's strengths and weaknesses. We believed in each other. I began to appreciate the spirit behind our motto, "We Believe," was grounded in hard work and preparation by our coaches and team—not simply on hope. We had learned how to win, as Coach Chmara urged us to do when we stood at 0–3. Except for the 39–6 win over Gary High School, our wins had not come easily. A total of seven points accounted for our other three wins. At this point of the season, I now played the role of a team leader for the first time in my football career. Who would have thought the second team fullback at Central Junior High merely three years ago would end up in this position?

The local sportswriters, especially Virgil L. "Stubby" Currence, wrote about our team daily. I grew up reading about the high school athletes in our area, and now I opened the morning paper to read articles about our team … and me. It was exciting to gain some recognition, but many people still regarded our team as the weakest Bluefield team of the past twenty years. We wanted to change that perception. We still faced two tough games on our remaining schedule. If we could win those games, it would help us demonstrate just how much we had improved over the past eight weeks.

In our final home game, we hosted East Bank, the defending state champions. On Friday morning of the game, one of our offensive and defensive standouts, Joe Hager, got into some minor trouble at school for goofing off. For reasons never fully explained, Joe ended up in our team's rolling laundry cart in the classroom of a teacher while her class was in session. The teacher complained to Coach Chmara. As a disciplinary measure, but mostly to appease the teacher, he benched Joe for the entire first quarter of the game. That's the last thing we needed when facing a quality team from the Charleston area. Trailing 17–6 at the start of the fourth quarter and 17–14 late in the game, we blocked a punt and Brian Bruckner scooped up the ball and returned it for a touchdown to lift us to another close, late game win 21–17.

With a 5–4 record, at a minimum, we had avoided a losing season. Our team took a lot of pride in winning five of our last six games. Stubby offered his opinion that this might have been Coach Chmara's finest coaching effort considering how the season began.

After a bye week, we finished our 1974 season at Pulaski County High School in southwest Virginia. Pulaski's student body was over twice the size of our school, and their team featured an outstanding running back who had committed to play at Virginia Tech. They presented yet another challenging team on our schedule that year. If we had played Pulaski earlier in the season, it is likely we would have lost. But we now held a certain degree of confidence in ourselves. We wanted to end the season on a high note, especially for the four seniors on our team who would be playing their final game. I scored two touchdowns and rushed for 175 yards, the most for a single game in my career, in a 27–14 victory.

Post-season Honors

I ended the 1974 season with eleven touchdowns and three two-point conversions for a total of 72 points. That put me in fifth place among the final area scoring leaders, but all four players ahead of me were either from Virginia or smaller schools in West Virginia. In addition, I finished with 1,035 rushing yards on 142 carries, nearly all of which came in the last seven games of the season. About two weeks after the season ended, I learned I had been named one of the first-team All-Area running backs. Considering I did not even start two of our first three games, earning post-season honors seemed highly unlikely only a few weeks earlier. Two other juniors from Bluefield made the All-Area team, Joe Hager and Rocky Malimisura, both at offensive line.

With the season behind us, we immediately started into off-season weightlifting and conditioning. Yes … time to return to the back room. Surprisingly, I looked forward to it. With almost our entire team returning in 1975, we willingly put in the work necessary during the off-season to get bigger and stronger.

The all-state football team was to be announced in the Sunday paper the weekend before Christmas. On Saturday evening, I was at the home of Julie, a girl I had started dating at the end of the football season. Julie's dad asked me what I thought about my chances to be on the all-state team. I said, "I hope to make honorable mention and perhaps third team with any luck."

He replied, "I am sure the Sunday paper has already been printed. Let's go to the Daily Telegraph office and pick one up." So, we hopped into his car and drove downtown shortly before midnight. He went into the office and returned with the Sunday edition. Opening the paper to the sports section, I saw my name listed as second team all-state running back. Excited and stunned, it was a surreal moment which I will never forget. The past three months had transformed my life. In that short period of time, I had gone from struggling for a starting position to being named one of the top running backs in the state. Incredible.

In addition to exceeding my expectations, being named second team all-state made me even more determined to avoid a letdown in 1975. All three first team running backs on the 1974 all-state team were underclassmen. We faced two of them in 1974, Walter Easley of Stonewall Jackson and Mike Lewis of Beckley. The third spot went to a sophomore from South Charleston named Robert Alexander. As fate would have it, we would face all three of them in 1975.

My football goals to this point of my life had been relatively simple … make the team and earn some playing time. I had not contemplated the thought of being a leader on a team with high expectations for the following season. I was not alone. Coach Chmara expected all the seniors to demonstrate leadership. He did not name permanent captains for that reason. Instead, he rotated captains on a game-by-game basis. Fortunately, our rising senior class collectively demonstrated the leadership skills he sought. Each one of us recalled the lessons of 1973. We took nothing for granted. Our class was committed to making the next season memorable.

Preparing for the Future

One day in January 1975, I received a letter from the U.S. Naval Academy letting me know I was on their list of potential football recruits. It was the first of several letters I would receive from colleges over the next few months. However, this first letter took me by surprise as I had not given much thought to the college recruiting process or even considered myself as a potential college player. Five months earlier, I was not even sure I could play for Bluefield, much less a college. I certainly had not contemplated what it meant to be a college football recruit. As far as I knew, most of the former Bluefield players who had continued to play at the collegiate level attended either WVU or local colleges. A few had played out-of-state at Division II colleges. Over the course of the next year, I learned that receiving an introductory letter did not equate to being offered a scholarship or even being recruited by that school. It simply indicated a possible interest. Nevertheless, as a sixteen-year-old high school player, I treasured each one I received. It allowed me to entertain the possibility of playing football beyond high school.

As we ground our way through the cold days of winter, my teammates and I dedicated ourselves to the conditioning program. If we failed in the upcoming fall '75 season, it would not be for lack of effort in the off-season. One day, during backroom workouts, Coach Ferrell grabbed a nearby broom and started using it as a motivational tool to playfully slap guys on the backside as a way to push them along during the workout. It was harmless and in fun. The next day, while we waited to start our workout, someone decided it would be a good idea to hide the broom and hope Coach Ferrell forgot about it. I tossed the broom into the overhead mechanical pipes, and it somehow stayed balanced on one of the pipes. Coach Ferrell showed up shortly thereafter and started the workout. Apparently, he had forgotten about the broom. He never used a broom in workouts prior to the previous session. Why would he remember it?

Then suddenly, one of the guys, Jim Hyder, laughingly asked Coach Ferrell, "Where's your broom?" Without hesitation, I decided to retrieve the broom and hope I could put it back on the floor before Coach Ferrell saw it. I jumped up, grabbed the broom handle, and flung it off the pipe. Just as I did so, Hyder pointed out the hidden location of the broom. Coach Ferrell looked up just in time for the broom handle to hit him squarely in the face. After we all enjoyed a good laugh for about five seconds, the rest of the workout went downhill quickly for me. We usually split into two groups and alternated doing conditioning drills for about sixty seconds. One group rested while the other group worked out. On this day, I alone comprised my own group. My turn lasted about sixty seconds, while the other groups' turns lasted about ten seconds. I could not wait for the session to finally end. Walking back to our lockers, several of my teammates told me how much they admired my effort. I think each one, in his own way, was saying to me, "I am glad it was you who hit Coach Ferrell and not me!"

The spring of my junior year remains one of my favorite times of high school. It was a time when I looked forward with anticipation to my upcoming senior year, but I did not feel compelled to put too much thought into the days beyond that ... days that would include leaving home and not seeing my friends daily. There would be time for that later. For now, I was content to enjoy the moment.

Back to Track

Those of us in the conditioning program eagerly awaited March 1, the start of track season, solely because that date signaled the end of winter conditioning. I enjoyed the chance to get outside again, and track practice lacked intensity. Unlike football practice and winter conditioning, the coaches provided minimal oversight at track practice. Coach Beckett gave us plenty of freedom and trusted we would each do whatever we needed to do to get ready for our events. My friends and I mostly performed stretching exercises for the first half of practice. After stretching for twenty minutes or so, we then practiced clearing hurdles or exchanging the baton for sprint relays. We did nothing I would consider taxing or difficult, and then we headed back to the locker room. We spent more time goofing off than we did running. Luckily, most of us were already in great shape and our halfhearted efforts at practice did not hurt us in track meets.

Some of my favorite springtime memories involved going on road trips for invitational track meets. The meets always started early on Saturday which required us to spend Friday night in a hotel. That's an experience we did not get to enjoy for football games. Since our track team consisted of only a couple dozen guys, we traveled in two fifteen-passenger vans rather than a bus. Coach

Beckett did not mind playing the hit tunes of the 70s on the radio while he drove the van, and we all sang along.

I qualified for the state track meet as part of the 400-meter, 800-meter, and hurdle relay teams. The state track meet began on Friday evening with qualifying events and then wrapped up on Saturday. The timing required us to stay in a hotel in Charleston on Friday night. By chance, our eleventh-grade chemistry teacher, Jim Kyle, was staying in the same hotel that evening on his last night as a bachelor. Mr. Kyle had recently graduated from West Virginia University, and while waiting to start medical school in the fall, he was substituting for our regular chemistry teacher, who was out on maternity leave. David Litz, Joey Beckett, and I decided he would likely welcome us dropping by his room to say hello. We obtained his room number from the front desk and went to see him. We knocked on his door only to learn we had interrupted a bachelor party. He was going out in style on his pre-wedding night with a roomful of college friends. That night represented my first interaction with totally wasted college-age individuals. Innocence is lost gradually.

Summer Highlights

Shortly after the school year ended, two of my favorite teachers, Eleanor Rupp and Rosanna Reaser, chaperoned our Bible Club on a week-long trip to Atlanta for a seminar called Institute in Basic Life Principles. A gentleman named Bill Gothard led the seminar which originated from his work with young people in Chicago. The sessions ran from six-thirty to nine o'clock nightly and then all day on Friday and Saturday. During the day, we explored Atlanta and went to Six Flags over Georgia. We had a great time! My initial reason for going on the trip was simply to have fun in Atlanta, but after the first session, I could not wait to return the following evening. Mr. Gothard spoke about self-acceptance, purpose, identity, topics that any high-schooler, or anyone for that matter, would find interesting.

The week after the Gothard seminar, I attended a leadership camp in northern West Virginia with three of my good friends, Martin Jarrell, Joe Hager, and Mark Powell. The U.S. Army supervised the camp, called Camp Dawson. I think the camp's purpose involved introducing basic Army leadership principles to rising high school seniors, but honestly, the purpose was never clear to me. We slept in barracks, rose at dawn, marched, and did conditioning exercises—as if I needed more physical conditioning.

Back in Bluefield by mid-June, I returned to work at the City Park. The second summer proved to be even easier than the first since we now knew the minimum level of effort required. Hanging out with my friends at City Park all day made for a perfect summer job. In the evenings, most of us attended voluntary workouts at the high school. We lifted weights, ran, and played catch. Nothing too strenuous. Just staying in shape and staying in touch with each other.

After a family vacation in late July, the start of football practice neared. I went to the barber for a short haircut before donning my helmet and other gear. One of my friends, Joe Hager, went a step further by shaving his head with a "B" on top. His picture was in the Daily Telegraph, and all of us at the evening workout enjoyed a good laugh over it. Later that evening, after our workout ended, he decided to shave the "B" off the top of his head to make his hair all one length—zero inches. Some of us thought it would be fun to watch, so we left the school and drove to Robert Lee's house where Robert produced an electric shaver. When you get a group of seventeen-year-old guys together in a room, male hormones can take over and stop the brain from functioning properly. After urging each other on, before I knew it, about ten of us had shaved our heads. I totally succumbed to peer pressure, but my friends certainly appreciated my participation.

Two of my teammates went home with me to see my parents' reaction. We were all laughing and having a good time until my mom and dad saw me. By the looks on their faces, I could tell they did not find it nearly as amusing as the rest of us. Dad's first question was, "How do you think that will look in your senior pictures?" Now that is a question I had not stopped to consider. After my friends departed, it finally sunk in—I had no hair. My mom basically grounded me. She made me stay home the next day to get some sun on my head while stringing green beans. Some of the other guys went swimming and ended up with sunburned scalps. For the next few weeks, I never went anywhere in public without wearing a cap or hat.

The next time Coach Chmara saw me, he said, "I understand some of those guys shaving their hair, but I thought you were smarter than that." Oh well, I guess not.

The length of my hair, or the lack of it, would soon be a moot point. My final year of football at Bluefield High was about to begin.

1975 Bluefield Beavers Football Team

1975 Cheerleaders, Karen Noble and Harriet Edwards seated.

Donnie and Joey Beckett warming up for a track meet.

Taking the field just before kickoff.

Slicing through the East Bank defense.

Sweeping right after handoff from Joey Beckett, #19.

Beaver fans display their opinion prior to state semi-final game.

Looking for running room against South Charleston.

Celebrating 1975 state title.

Head Coach, John Chmara

Sportswriter,
Virgil L. "Stubby" Currence

Dream fulfilled.

Chapter Six

One Final Chance
Senior Year, 1975–1976

Preseason practices in August 1975 turned out to be much more tolerable than 1974. Two new coaches joined our staff, Chuck Martin and Steve Bourne. Both were splendid additions and contributed greatly to our 1975 team. Coach Martin became a trusted sounding board for me in the recruiting process later that fall and winter. Ironically, he saw only two or three of our games that season in person due to the fact his job entailed scouting our opponent for the following week. That task required him to attend the game of the school coming up next on our schedule. Coach Bourne had played quarterback for Bluefield a few years earlier, and he showed more empathy with the current players.

Our coaches chose to return to a more reasonable end-of-practice conditioning session rather than four sessions per practice. That did not mean they made practices easy … just easier than the prior year. We still worked hard. With so many returning starters, we already knew our basic offense and defense. That allowed us to spend more time perfecting our execution. Coach Chmara thrived on execution! We would run the same play over and over repeatedly in practice until he was satisfied every single player knew exactly what to do.

Accordingly, we developed a sense of the importance of teamwork early and often. We supported and encouraged one another realizing we must all play at a high standard to field a strong team. That team-first attitude resulted in fervent support for each other both on and off the field.

We required no extra motivation at preseason practice that year. In four weeks, we would face the defending state champions on the road in our first game. Our team returned a solid core of seniors: Rocky Malimisura, Joey Beckett, Joe Hager, Robert Lee, Brian Bruckner, Jaycee Collins, Jeff Simmons, Randy Albert, Kelvin Haden, Tommy Goforth, Martin Jarrell, Jeb Blevins, Mark Powell, David McGlothlin, Mike McHaffa, Randy Kiser, Greg James, and Jim Hyder. The junior class included some key contributors such as Ronaldo Holland and Brent Sizemore, who both started on our offensive line. The sophomore class included a future star in Wayne Baumgardner. Wayne became a two-way starter early in preseason practice at right end on offense and free safety on defense.

From day one of practice, we focused on the season opening matchup at Stonewall Jackson on August 29, 1975. As previously noted, Stonewall Jackson won the 1974 AAA state championship and had beaten us 26–0 at Mitchell Stadium my junior year. Like us, their team consisted of many returning key seniors. They were overwhelming favorites to repeat as state champions in 1975. The stakes could not have been any higher for a season opener. The dreams for our entire season would depend heavily on the outcome of our very first game, played in Charleston on their home field. As I said, we were sufficiently motivated.

Coach Chmara taught the game of football. He did not scream. He did not display a lot of emotion. He required us to display good sportsmanship and respect our opponents. When we scored a touchdown, he expected the person scoring to hand the ball back to the officials. He wanted the person scoring to act like this was not the first time he had ever seen the end zone. He often addressed us as "gentlemen" prior to giving us instructions. When he disliked the outcome of something, he went to his standard curse word of "horseshit." As in, "Horseshit. Run that play again." Or "Horseshit, son. Don't you know who to block?"

Of course, there was no correct answer to a question like that. If you said, "No, sir," then you would be chastised for not knowing your assignment, resulting in the entire team being required to run the exact same play repeatedly until Coach Chmara was satisfied. If you said, "Yes, sir," then you would likely hear Coach Chmara reply, "Well then, why don't you block him? A chain is only as strong at its weakest link. Don't be the weak link, son." He used that phrase quite often.

Coach Chmara displayed a sense of confidence and control which filtered down to us. He expected to win every game, and he conducted himself accordingly. He possessed a remarkable ability to design a game plan to specifically address the strengths and weaknesses of each of our opponents. He inserted new plays and made defensive adjustments prior to each game on our schedule. With an entire summer to prepare for Stonewall Jackson, he held nothing back. I don't think we could have been any better prepared.

A Huge Game to Start the Season

Friday, August 29, finally arrived. In the morning newspaper, I saw most of the sportswriters favored Stonewall Jackson to win by at least fourteen points. That did not surprise me.

Our school year had not yet started, so I tried to relax at home that morning. The clock seemed to stand still. I wanted to get to the locker room, pack my gear, and get on the road. Our team met at the high school around noon for the slightly over two-hour bus ride to Laidley Field in Charleston. I had been to three football games at Laidley Field: the 1962 and 1965 AAA state championship games, and the 1972 semifinal playoff game. Therefore, I associated this stadium with important games. Tonight's game would be no exception, but tonight, I would be playing rather than watching.

Stepping off our air-conditioned bus, the heat and humidity of the early evening hit us smack in the face. After arriving for an away game, we put our gear into the visiting locker room, as usual. Then we spent a few minutes walking around the field prior to putting on our uniforms. Located in the Kanawha River Valley, Charleston typically experienced warmer temperatures than Bluefield, but that Friday seemed unusually hot, and the heavy air felt suffocating. I found it a little difficult to breathe, although that may have been a factor of my nerves as much as the weather.

90

Maroon & White

As game time approached, we exited the locker room for our pregame warmup. Seeing Stonewall Jackson take the field for their pregame routine in their bright red jerseys with matching silver helmets and silver pants made the reality of the moment set in. The game we had embraced as our motivation throughout all our workouts and practices over the last nine months was at hand.

Feeling completely opposite of my enthusiasm of the morning, I now wanted time to stand still. Things were moving too quickly. My excitement to start the season was tempered by my apprehension of our own hopes for our entire season ending quickly if we lost this game. The final minutes leading up to kickoff ticked by. Ready or not, we were about to find out how we stacked up against the defending state champions.

We received the opening kickoff and could not move the ball. We punted to Stonewall Jackson, and they took possession near midfield. We designed our defense for the game primarily to stop Walter Easley, their all-state running back, but apparently no one informed him. On Stonewall's first series, Easley broke loose for a fifty-yard touchdown run, and they quickly led 6–0. The game could not have started any worse for us. We could not move the ball. They scored a long touchdown on their first series of the game. Doubts about our ability to compete immediately crept into our minds.

Sensing this, Coach Chmara knew we must respond or else we risked falling out of contention early. He decided to resort to one of the special plays designed specifically for this game. Starting at our own twenty-yard line, we flipped our unbalanced line from its usual right of center formation to the left, intending to confuse

Stonewall's defense. Brian Bruckner, normally the left end, lined up as a wide receiver on the right hash mark, and I lined up as a flanker in the slot next to him. After the snap, Brian stepped back a couple of yards to catch a lateral pass from our quarterback, Joey. Then, Brian threw the ball deep downfield where I managed to catch it while outmaneuvering their defensive back who missed the ball and then missed the tackle. All of this combined action resulted in me covering the remaining distance to the end zone untouched. Brian then added the extra point, putting us ahead 7–6 in the first quarter. That single play boosted our morale and gave us some much-needed confidence. Although the outcome of the game was enormously in doubt and would not be determined for another three and a half quarters, we now sensed this game would be a battle for the entire four quarters. The months-long preparation by our coaching staff resulted in a brilliant play call at a critical moment of the game, and ultimately our season.

Both defenses settled in after those back-to-back scoring plays until midway through the second quarter when I scored again on a sixty-eight-yard trap play designed to go right up the middle. As usual, Joe Hager made a great block allowing me to get quickly into the secondary and race down the right sideline for the score. We led at halftime 13–6. The heat remained stifling. Since I played both ways and returned punts and kicks, I did not have time to drink fluids on the sideline. At halftime, I tried to drink as much as I could which turned out to be enough to prevent me from getting leg cramps that night.

After kicking off to Stonewall to start the second half, we forced them to punt. We called for a "punt return right" which meant Jeff Simmons was supposed to return the punt. I lined up on the right hash, and Jeff lined up on the left hash at about our twenty-yard line. If I caught the ball, I would hand it to Jeff on a reverse. If Jeff caught the ball, he would fake a reverse to me and continue down the right sideline. However, the punt turned out to be short and to the far right which required me to run forward, almost to the sideline, to field the ball. At this point, I would have had to give up yardage to get the ball into Jeff's hands since he was several yards behind me. Therefore, after catching the ball, I instinctively kept running down the right sideline. In the moment, I intended to simply pick up as many yards as I could to give us better field position. However, with all the blocking already in place for a "return right," there was a clear opening. I would need to avoid just one defender—Walter Easley, the punter. I faked to the right and stepped back to the left as Easley missed the tackle. A sixty-nine-yard punt return gave us a 19–6 lead early in the third quarter. The Bluefield side of the stadium buzzed with excitement, but Stonewall Jackson realized they were in trouble, and they were not going down without a fight.

On their next possession, Stonewall drove sixty yards for a touchdown reducing our lead to 19–12, going into the fourth quarter.

After we failed to pick up a first down, we punted the ball back to Stonewall, allowing them a chance to initiate a potentially game-winning drive. Midway through the fourth quarter, we incurred an extremely costly penalty. Not only did it give Stonewall a first down, but it removed our best linebacker from the game. The officials flagged Joe Hager for a spearing penalty and ejected him from the game. Joe may have been slightly late on the tackle, but it certainly did not warrant ejection from the game in my opinion. Regardless, we had to deal with it. Our defense had kept Stonewall's high powered offense mostly in check, but we now needed to stop them at least one more time without one of our key defensive leaders.

Stonewall continued their drive, reaching our ten-yard line with first-and-goal. Due to the fact we had scored all our touchdowns quickly on explosive plays, our defense had been on the field for a significant part of the evening. Our defensive starters were tired, but everyone was giving it their all. I have learned it is much more stressful to watch a close game than to play in one. When you are on the field, you think only about the next play and your assignment. You have no time to contemplate all possible outcomes. With a crucial victory so near, we needed to overcome our fatigue and find a way to stop their drive. In the huddle, we encouraged each other to dig deep for one more play. Through a great team effort, we managed to stop Stonewall at the two-yard line on fourth down.

We took possession with about two minutes left in the game. Although we had kept Stonewall out of the end zone, we had no margin for error. Our offense lined up with our backs literally in the end zone. We knew it was important to hold on to the football and not turn it back over to Stonewall on a fumble. We needed at least one first down to secure the win. Fortunately, we were able to pick up a couple of first downs and maintain our drive long enough to allow us to run out the clock by kneeling the final plays of the game. After finishing the game with over three-hundred total rushing, receiving, and return yards. I felt a deep sense of satisfaction walking off the field that evening.

We had secured the biggest win of our high school career and proven the predictions wrong. By knocking off the defending state champions, we also sent a message to the rest of the AAA teams in the state—Bluefield was once again a team to be reckoned with. I cannot overstate the importance of that victory to our season. Without it, the opportunity to play in another game of that magnitude may not have come.

In addition to feeling satisfied, I felt extremely thirsty. I should have been drinking water all day prior to the game and certainly after the game. Our post-game meal generally consisted of fried chicken and a can of Coke. One twelve-ounce can of Coke only served to increase my thirst for the entire ride back to Bluefield. The next morning, I weighed myself on our scales. My normal weight was around one-hundred seventy-five pounds. I weighed about ten pounds less than normal. I drank plenty of water and fluids that day to restore my weight.

The headline of the Saturday sports page read, "Beavers Shock Stonewall Jackson 19–12—Jackson Scores Three Touchdowns." The outcome justified all the hard work, the winter conditioning, the summer workouts, the preseason training, and losing a few pounds of water weight.

Nine More to Go

The victory over Stonewall certainly represented a huge win, but we still had to play nine more teams. Next up, our cross-town rival Graham. Graham returned several players from the team that won the 1974 area championship. We knew many of their players. A couple of them, Rick Marrs and Buster Large, even worked with us at the city park during the summer. Despite the coaches and the newspaper trying to predict this as a close game, I certainly believed we would avenge the prior year's loss.

We wasted no time in putting the game away. We scored on our first possession and several others in a 48–0 win. We led 22–0 at halftime. I returned the second half kickoff eighty-eight yards for a touchdown. After that, the reserves played the rest of game.

The following week we faced Princeton at home. No one on our team doubted we would complete the sweep of the teams that had defeated us the first three games of last season. Princeton came into the game with a 2–0 record, but they had played weaker competition, and we felt good about the fact we nearly beat them in 1974. I felt extremely confident we would win this game by a large margin. We were heavily favored.

As we put on our uniforms that evening, I recall discussing my concerns about the game with some of my teammates. Of course, my concerns did not include whether we would win or lose the game. On the contrary, my biggest concern, along with most of my teammates, was that Coach Chmara would pull the starters from the game too early and not allow us to run up the score against the Tigers. As it turned out, we gave Coach Chmara no choice. The starters played the entire game.

Princeton established the tone for the game early by scoring on its opening possession to take an 8–0 lead. *Okay, that was a fluke*, I told myself. We immediately answered on our first play following Princeton's score just like we had done against Stonewall Jackson. However, this time, no trickery was needed. I scored on an eighty-yard touchdown run made easy by the huge hole our offensive line created. We scored once again in the first quarter and added a third touchdown early in the second quarter to extend our lead to 22–8. The rout was on ... so I thought.

Princeton refused to fold. I give their coach, Coach Pack, a lot of credit for keeping his team in the game after falling behind. Princeton scored another touchdown before the first half ended to make the score 22–14. We could not get our offense going in the third quarter, but Princeton scored once again to reduce our lead to an uncomfortably close 22–20. I definitely had not considered the possibility this game would be remotely close going into the fourth quarter. Princeton now had our full attention. With the momentum clearly in Princeton's favor, we finally put together a sustained drive which ended in my fourth touchdown of the night to make the score 28–20. Princeton tried to answer with one final drive deep into our territory as time wound down. On the final play of the game, Kelvin Haden intercepted a pass in the end zone and the officials generously gave Princeton a safety on the tackle making the final score 28–22.

The Daily Telegraph called the game "one of the most spectacular games played here." *Spectacular* is not the word I would have chosen, but it certainly turned out to be more exciting than most people anticipated. It had not been easy, but we had reversed our 0–3 start from 1974.

After three games, I easily topped the list of area scoring leaders in 1975 with fifty-six points scored. The next closest player checked in with twenty-two points. Many articles in the Bluefield Daily Telegraph started comparing me to some of the great Beaver running backs I had grown up admiring, such as Pete Wood. I came into my senior year hoping to improve upon my junior season, but this type of start even took me by surprise. I enjoyed the fact that many people in our area now recognized my name. However, I never lost sight of the truth that it takes an entire team, including coaches, to win. Football is a team game. Success requires the execution of all eleven players on the field. Coach Chmara had successfully ingrained that concept in all of us. I did my part—worked hard at practice, studied game films, studied scouting reports, and whatever else I thought would help us win.

We easily overmatched our next two opponents, Oak Hill at home and Gary on the road, by scores of 40–13 and 40–0, respectively, to run our record to 5–0. The starters barely played in the second half of either game. I added another four touchdowns to my season total. More importantly, we moved into the state rankings at number eight and were in position to vie for one of the four playoff spots.

Looking ahead at our schedule, Woodrow Wilson of Beckley loomed large in a mere two weeks. After an undefeated 1974 season, Beckley suffered a 3-point loss to St. Albans at the start of the 1975 season. Led by returning all-state running back Mike Lewis, Beckley had lost only two games in three years. They had beaten us soundly 38–14 a year earlier. We could not help but look ahead to that game, despite the fact we faced one more opponent before then—Welch.

Something Unexpected

A mining town near the coal fields of West Virginia, Welch possessed a rich football tradition. We had defeated them in a closely contested game, 19–18, in 1974. But since we returned more starters, and we had already defeated higher quality teams in 1975, we fully expected to win. I scored a touchdown early in the game from one yard out, and despite missing the extra point, I thought we would cruise to another easy win. However, Welch responded with a touchdown of their own and converted their two-point attempt for an 8–6 lead. Other than the opening drive, our offense remained ineffective. Welch, on the other hand, made the plays necessary to keep drives alive and control the clock. Normally our four defensive linemen and four linebackers controlled the line of scrimmage. But on this night, the Welch running backs consistently found their way into our secondary. Wayne, Kelvin, and I were required to make more than our normal share of tackles. I urged our defensive tackles to step up and make some stops. But all I heard in reply was, "They are holding us." The officials apparently did not think so. No penalties were called.

As the game wore on, Welch added another score and now led 14–6. We desperately needed to score. We finally got our offense going at that critical moment with a long drive deep into Welch territory. On first and goal from inside the ten-yard line, Jaycee Collins ripped through an opening to the one-yard line. With three downs remaining, I felt certain we would score a touchdown and two-point conversion to tie the game. After all, we had won eleven of our last twelve games going back to the previous season, and we had consistently made the plays we needed to make during that stretch. However, after coming up short attempting quarterback sneaks on both second and third downs, we now faced fourth down in a must-score situation. I lined up at tailback, and Jaycee and Jeff lined up as blockers in what we called a Power-I Right formation. I am reasonably sure everyone in the stadium, including Welch's defense, knew who would be carrying the ball and where. As mentioned previously, Coach Chmara liked to say every play is designed to score a touchdown if every player executes his job. Unfortunately, we missed an assignment on this play. As soon as Joey handed the ball to me, an unblocked defensive tackle, who later played at WVU, wrapped his rather large arms around me and tackled me for no gain short of the goal line.

As I watched the final seconds tick off the scoreboard clock, the chilly night air only served to accentuate the feeling of helplessness. We had lost.

After the game, we were in a state of shock as we showered and dressed in the visiting locker room for the return to Bluefield. Our promising season now lay in ruins. Our hopes and dreams unexpectedly crushed on October 3, 1975. I felt sick all night and the following Saturday. My mom and dad tried to cheer me up, but I was not yet ready for that. What had gone wrong? How could we have lost this game at this point of the season? I could not get my mind around the answers to those questions.

After watching the game film Sunday afternoon, the answers became more apparent. Not only did Welch's offensive line hold our defensive linemen, they essentially tackled our defenders on many plays creating huge holes for their running backs to get into our secondary. By doing so, Welch kept their drives alive and kept our offense off the field. Welch ran nearly twice as many offensive plays during the game as we did, and they controlled the time of possession. Nonetheless, officiating is part of the game, and we could only blame ourselves for failing to score on the crucial series of downs late in the fourth quarter. We simply had not overcome the adversity we faced that night. We did not make any big plays as we had become accustomed to doing in our previous games of the season.

I was held to fifty-five yards rushing on a handful of carries—the lowest output of any game since early in my junior year when I had been limited with a broken hand.

Without a doubt, we now truly faced a do-or-die game against Beckley. The loser would be eliminated from any chance of making the playoffs ... and the winner would still need some help.

Coach Chmara did not dwell on the loss, and he did not let us remain mired in self-pity. He said, "That one is in the books. There isn't anything we can do to change it. We must concentrate on Beckley." He focused our attention on Beckley's high-powered offense and stout defense. By Monday afternoon, we put the Welch loss behind us and began preparations for hosting Beckley on Friday night.

A Must-Win Game

The loss to Welch knocked us out of the top ten in the state rankings. Beckley came into the game ranked eighth with a 4–1 record. Despite the loss to Welch, or perhaps due to it, a heightened level of intensity filled the week leading up to the game. The buildup in the local papers exceeded even the normal level of hype. The headlines in Beckley's daily newspaper included "Eagles Must Stop Jackson" and "Flying Eagles, Bluefield Meet in Pivotal Game Tonight." Of course, the Beckley paper picked Beckley to win by six points. The Bluefield paper echoed the importance of the matchup: "Bluefield Hosts Eagles in Crucial Game." Both coaches respected one another. Both teams knew this game essentially served as an elimination game for the playoff picture.

We responded with possibly our best game of the entire season.

We forced Beckley to punt on their first possession, and after returning the punt to Beckley's thirty-eight-yard line, I scored a few plays later for a 7–0 lead. I scored again early in the second quarter to increase our lead to 13–0. Then Joey connected with Wayne Baumgardner for a twelve-yard touchdown, and Martin Jarrell returned a Beckley fumble fifty yards for a touchdown to break the game open. Meanwhile, our defense continued to keep Beckley's offense in check. Somewhat stunned, but in a good way, and in disbelief, we ended the first half with a 27–0 lead. I guess it's safe to say the loss at Welch had sharpened our focus. We did not let up. We increased our lead to 34–0 early in the third quarter and totally dominated the game in a 50–14 win. Stubby Currence's coverage of the contest stated he had never seen a Beaver team so completely outplay a good football team. That statement said a lot since Stubby had worked for the Bluefield Daily Telegraph for over four decades, and he had seen all the great Beaver teams of the past. The win moved us back into the state rankings at number eight behind Buckhannon-Upshur, Parkersburg South, Parkersburg, Ravenswood, Charleston, South Charleston, and East Bank. With three games remaining, at least we had returned to the playoff conversation. Some of the teams ahead of us, such as Parkersburg South and Parkersburg, would face each other as the season wound down, and we could knock off East Bank ourselves in two weeks.

Climbing Back into the Playoff Picture

Coming off a highly emotional game, there is always the risk of a letdown the following week. But we fully understood we could not afford any letdown. We hosted a well-coached, challenging Greenbrier East team on October 17, 1975. Greenbrier East came into the game with a 5–1 record, having suffered their one loss to Beckley by six points earlier in the season. A steady downpour and muddy field conditions throughout the game hampered both teams. Fortunately, we got off to a great start when I returned the opening kickoff eighty-five yards for a touchdown. As an added benefit, I kept my white uniform unmuddied for at least one more play. That did not last long. We scored on a seventy-six-yard drive on our next possession and then played the rest of the evening with a view of holding on to the ball and getting the game over as quickly as possible. Coach Chmara credited the opening kickoff return as a significant factor in our 22–6 win since it gave us a quick lead on a night when weather conditions made scoring difficult.

Due to the rainy weather that evening, we all brought our maroon-colored parkas to the game. With a hood, the parkas wrapped our entire uniform from our helmet to our knee-length socks. They helped keep players on the sidelines somewhat warm and dry. Since I spent little time on the sideline, I left mine in the home locker room. As we boarded the bus after the game to head back to the school, I saw Coach Ferrell walking down the aisle carrying a parka. He found me and asked, "Is this yours?"

With number 18 plainly embroidered on the sleeve, the question was obviously rhetorical. I knew exactly what this meant. The rules applied to everyone. No exceptions. The only thing I could say in response was, "Thanks for grabbing that for me."

He handed it to me with a sly grin and said what I knew he would say, "See you at six-thirty Monday."

With the win, we moved up two spots to number six in the state rankings. It is worth pointing out that Princeton also moved into the rankings at number eight with an identical 7–1 record. Looking back at our close game with them in September, it now made more sense that we had not overpowered them. Also, Princeton had recently defeated Welch, something we were unable to do.

With nineteen touchdowns and a total of one-hundred sixteen points, my lead on the list of area scoring leaders nearly doubled the next closest player. However, my points merely reflected our team's success. Genuine excitement filled the air in late October … another byproduct of our success. Both at school and around town, people shared in our enthusiasm and anticipation of how our season would play out. We stood in the midst of making memories in 1975 that would last for the rest of our lives. At times, I found it difficult to stay focused on academics, but I managed. After football practice, I had little time to do anything other than eat dinner and complete my homework.

We traveled back to the Kanawha River Valley, south of Charleston, for our next game at East Bank. They had lost their second game of the season the prior week and dropped out of the top ten, but they still presented a challenging test. The seniors on our team clearly recalled losing a critical game at East Bank near the end of our sophomore season. We could not let that happen again. Our fans traveled in full force to support us as always. Without doubt, seeing familiar faces in the stands and seeing our cheerleaders on the sideline made away games feel more comfortable. The support of our community and classmates meant more than they realized. With each game now in effect representing a playoff elimination game, we deeply appreciated their support.

We kicked off and East Bank fumbled inside their own fifteen-yard line. With a short field to negotiate, I covered the final ten yards quickly, and we led 6–0. Our defense held East Bank to three downs and a punt on their next possession. I returned the punt forty-five yards to the East Bank twenty-five-yard line. With another short field, Joey scored soon after, and we led 14–0. By halftime, we had extended our lead to 29–0 removing any suspense regarding the outcome. We dominated the game both offensively and defensively and won handily 35–10.

In the Charleston paper the following day, the headline for the game unbelievably read, "East Bank Not Impressed with Bluefield." The article quoted their coach as saying, "Bluefield was not that good. We could have upset them. They are definitely not in the same class as Charleston or South Charleston." Talk about sour grapes. I would have been embarrassed to lose 35–10 and then go on a rant about the other team not being that good. What did that say about East Bank—the coach's own team? I think the Charleston sportswriter sarcastically made that same point in the article. As always, Coach Chmara handled it like a gentleman, saying "Interviewing a coach after a loss is not the best time."

With an 8–1 record, we now headed into our bye week before our final home game against Pulaski County, Virginia. We had climbed to number five in the state … one spot out of the playoffs behind top-ranked Buckhannon-Upshur, second-ranked Parkersburg South, third-ranked Charleston, and fourth-ranked South Charleston. Even though South Charleston's point rating of 13.1 barely exceeded our 13.0 rating, we could not pick up enough points even if we beat Pulaski County to overtake them or anyone else in the top four. Our only hope relied on one of the teams ahead of us losing one of their final two games.

None of them lost during our bye week.

We remained ranked fifth heading into our final game of the season. At this point, undefeated Buckhannon-Upshur and undefeated Parkersburg South had secured playoff spots even if they lost their final game. Both Charleston and South Charleston were favored over their unranked, last-game opponents.

Our Final Game … Or Not?

I begrudgingly accepted the fact our game against Pulaski County on November 7, 1975, would likely be my final game in a

Beaver uniform as we progressed through our normal Friday night ritual. I assumed our loss at Welch would epitomize the unforgivable blip on our season. The loss would turn out to be as devastating as it seemed at the time. Since we did not control our own destiny, we could do just one thing that night—win and hope for the best.

We took care of business quickly. I returned the opening kickoff eighty yards for a touchdown—the third time during the season I had returned a kickoff for a touchdown to open a half. On our next possession, I carried the ball on our first play from scrimmage seventy-three yards for another touchdown. I scored again on our third possession. We led 35–0 at the end of the first quarter. With three quarters remaining, the only question was whether we could exceed 100 points. But we knew Coach Chmara would never allow it. Despite our dominant senior night performance, I felt sad knowing this was the end.

Nonetheless, until we were officially eliminated, we held out a small degree of hope. As our reserves finished up the final three quarters, our thoughts on the sidelines turned to another game. Charleston was playing at Dupont, the team that ended Bluefield's last playoff trip in 1972. In the third quarter of our game, word spread to our bench from someone with a radio in the stands that Dupont was leading Charleston. The rumor spread quickly among our team, but we did not know whether to believe it or not. You know the thing with rumors … someone could have simply heard the score incorrectly. One report said Dupont led by twelve points. The next report said Dupont led by only one point. I honestly doubted the rumors were true but wishing for them to be true was better than the alternative.

It's funny, now that I think back on it, but I spent most of the evening during possibly the last game of my high school career on the sideline trying to keep up with a game ninety miles away. We won by a final score of 69–12. As we made our way back to the locker room, we learned from our fans that the game in Charleston had ended. Dupont had indeed defeated previously third-ranked Charleston 24–0. The loss would cause Charleston to drop in the rankings and we would move up to fourth place. That meant ...

WE WERE GOING TO THE STATE PLAYOFFS!

The excitement of that night was unforgettable. To be given a second chance after losing to Welch felt like a heavy weight had been lifted off our shoulders. Rather than ending our season as another one-loss Beaver team that missed the playoffs, we now would have a chance to bring Bluefield its first state title since 1967.

For the season, we outscored our opponents 357–103. I scored twenty-five touchdowns and a total of one hundred fifty-four points, easily the most in our area, but short of South Charleston's Robert Alexander for state scoring leader. Buckhannon-Upshur finished the regular season undefeated and ranked number one. The other three schools making the playoffs, Parkersburg South, South Charleston, and our team, all finished with a record of 9–1. The four-team format pitted number one against number four, and number two against number three. Thus, South Charleston would face Parkersburg South in one semifinal, and we would face Buckhannon-Upshur at Laidley Field in the other semifinal.

State Playoffs – Semifinal Game

We knew absolutely nothing about Buckhannon-Upshur. They played in northern West Virginia. Most of the teams in that area did not play often outside their region. However, one of the teams from that region had won the 1972 state championship. I assumed the Buck-Ups would be good. They were ranked first in the state, after all. Honestly, I did not care who we played. The opportunity to keep playing was all that mattered. After going through back-to-back 6–4 seasons and being precariously close to ending this season one spot short of the playoffs, a second chance energized all of us.

The entire student body buzzed with anticipation the following week. Many of them planned to make the trip to Charleston on Saturday. As always, our fan base could not have been more supportive.

By coincidence, Buckhannon Upshur's star running back shared my same last name. The Jackson versus Jackson comparisons provided easy headlines for the sportswriters in several articles leading up to the game that week.

Of course, our coaching staff installed a game plan specifically for Buckhannon-Upshur. Coach Chmara and his staff, Beckett, Ferrell, Martin, and Bourne had worked tirelessly throughout the season to prepare us for each game. With a playoff game looming, they worked even harder. We would have one extra day to prepare since the game would be played on Saturday afternoon instead of the usual game time of Friday night. Coach Chmara took full advantage of the extra time. By the end of the week, I honestly think I knew Buckhannon-Upshur's offense and defense as well as their own players did. That level of preparation, bestowed on us by our coaches, strengthened our conviction of coming out victorious.

We played the game on Saturday afternoon, November 15, 1975, in Charleston. We left Bluefield Saturday morning and arrived at Laidley Field a couple hours before kickoff. This being our third trip to Charleston in the last three months, the bus ride and preparation for the game now held a degree of familiarity. Our fans traveled in full force and completely packed the stands on our side of the field. Our cheerleaders, two Karens, Harriet, Beverly, and the rest occupied their usual spot near our bench. One of our fans hung a huge banner from the bleachers proclaiming in large print, "Our Jackson is better than your Jackson." I did not know if that statement would prove to be true, but I felt confident our team was better than their team and that's all that would matter at the end of the day. The sun shone brightly with slightly cold temperatures. Perfect football weather for mid-November.

Both teams opened the game conservatively to get into the flow. Neither team moved the ball effectively on its initial possessions. We forced Buckhannon to punt from deep inside their own territory, and I looked forward to establishing good field position on the punt return. As it turned out, no return was needed. We blocked the punt. Jim Hyder scooped up the ball and stepped into the end zone. I completed a two-point conversion pass to Wayne Baumgardner on a play we used often for extra point attempts where I could choose whether to run or pass. As a side note, we ran that particular play only for two-point conversion attempts. We never utilized it otherwise. Perhaps Coach Chmara did not have much confidence in my passing ability after all.

With an 8–0 lead, we continued to control the ball and the clock throughout the remainder of the first half. Buckhannon made a couple of first downs but never threatened to score. In the second quarter, our offense put together a sustained drive culminating in my first touchdown of the playoffs on a short two-yard run. We led by a margin of fifteen points at the half, but we had thoroughly outplayed Buckhannon, and I felt optimistic about our chances of winning.

Early in the second half, after forcing Buckhannon to punt, our offensive line opened another large hole in the defensive front which I slipped through for a sixty-nine-yard touchdown run. With their running game totally ineffective, Buckhannon decided to give their passing game a try. Huge mistake. From their own twenty-yard line, their quarterback overthrew his intended target, but he did not overthrow me. I easily intercepted the pass and followed a convoy of teammates into the end zone. With a 28–0 lead midway through the third quarter, the eventual outcome of the game was no longer in doubt. Our second team played most of the fourth quarter and we won handily 42–0. Our defense held Buckhannon to forty-eight yards rushing for the game. Coach Chmara instilled in us the belief that we should always expect to win. I did expect to win … but not that easily. After all, the Buck-Ups came into the game ranked number one. But that Saturday afternoon at Laidley Field proved to be much less difficult than our previous trip in late August when we faced Stonewall Jackson.

With the victory, we earned the right to play in the West

Virginia AAA state championship game for the first time since I was in the fourth grade. We would face South Charleston and its star running back, Robert Alexander. South Charleston had defeated Parkersburg South that same day by a score of 49–8. Alexander scored five touchdowns in their semifinal game as South Charleston piled up over four hundred yards of offense. We would undoubtedly face a more difficult challenge in the championship game than the game we had just played, regardless of state rankings.

Prior to the two semifinal games, the West Virginia High School Athletic Association announced that Mitchell Stadium, our home field, would host the AAA state championship game if Bluefield earned a spot in it. I guess they decided Bluefield had earned that right after traveling to either Charleston or Parkersburg for its previous four state championship matches. As a result, I would play my final high school game in Mitchell Stadium after all, certainly a deserving location. Years later, it was named the number one high school stadium in America by a USA Today poll.

The week leading up to the championship game passed by in a blur. Talk of the game dominated discussions at school, on the street, and in the Daily Telegraph, of course. Many businesses posted signs showing support and wishing us good luck. I knew Mitchell Stadium would be packed Saturday with not only people from Bluefield, but also with other interested football fans from the area who wanted to attend the largest high school sporting event in the stadium's history. Fans from other schools in our area attended the game; some to root for us and some to root against us. Either way was fine. The display of emotions by fans on both sides would contribute to the atmosphere. That is how a state championship game should be. Regardless, we knew our fans would turn out in force giving us a home field advantage.

The coaching staff again developed an excellent defensive game plan designed to stop South Charleston's vaunted rushing attack. Our offensive game plan remained essentially unchanged except for a couple of minor adjustments to our formations. Coach Chmara liked to show our opponents something they had not seen on film and therefore had not put into their game preparation. On Friday evening before the game, the players made a pact to call one another around eight o'clock as a way to hold each other accountable for being safe at home and focused on the game. Unlike the Stonewall Jackson game to start the season, I don't recall feeling nervous at all. We relished the opportunity to do something no Beaver team had done since 1967. Something that seemed out of reach just two short weeks ago.

State Championship Saturday

I remember waking up the morning of Saturday, November 22, 1975, and thinking, *"It's time to get up! Today is the day."* I would describe my feelings as excited. My dad, however, was nervous that morning. I could tell by the way he paced around the room as I ate breakfast. As I previously stated, those watching a game are usually more nervous than those playing. I understand that. The people outside the locker room cannot fully appreciate the level of planning and preparation for a game. I knew we were ready. I could not wait to exit our locker room in a few short hours to play for the state championship in front of a huge crowd in our home stadium.

South Charleston entered the game as a four-point favorite to win. Eight of the nine sportswriters in Charleston picked South Charleston. Dad made sure I read Stubby Currence's article in the Daily Telegraph that morning titled, "An Open Letter to our Lads." In it, Stubby basically expressed his belief in Coach Chmara and our team to make Bluefield proud. Stubby never wavered in his support.

Even though we did not face a two-hour bus ride like we did in the semifinal, we still arrived at the school early Saturday morning. We went through our normal pre-game routine, similar to the routine of any Friday home game. That routine always included some time in the school gym for players to be alone without any coaches in the room. Anyone who wanted to speak could do so during this time. That morning, we expressed our belief in each other. We had experienced many highs and lows together, especially our senior class, to get to this point. I could live with losing, but only if we gave our best effort and still came up short. Regardless of the outcome, we did not want to look back with any regrets. That's all we could do. I hoped it would be enough.

We arrived at Mitchell Stadium in our maroon-and-white school bus about an hour before kickoff. Unlike the previous Saturday, clouds blocked the sun and the temperatures hovered near freezing. Despite the gloomy weather, fans of both teams already filled the stands completely by the time we arrived. The attendance of twelve thousand fans far exceeded the stadium's seating capacity, forcing many people to stand along the fence surrounding the field or find a spot on the stadium's north bank near the scoreboard. Our uniforms for the day consisted of light silver pants and white jerseys with maroon trim to match our maroon helmets. South Charleston wore white pants, black jerseys with orange trim, and white helmets. Joe Hager and I represented our team as captains for this game with our remaining seniors acting as honorary captains. South Charleston won the toss and elected to receive.

Our defense had been outstanding the past several weeks, so I did not mind kicking off to open the game. However, the kick rolled out of bounds giving South Charleston the ball on their own forty-yard line. On the second play of the game, a poor exchange between the quarterback and Alexander resulted in a fumble. David McGlothlin recovered the ball to set us up on South Charleston's side of the field, but we turned the ball over on downs after failing to convert on fourth and one. On South Charleston's next possession, our defense forced another turnover. This time Martin Jarrell recovered the ball at the seventeen-yard line, but we again failed on fourth down. We could have tried for a field goal, but we always felt better about our chances to convert on fourth down than we did kicking. Remarkably, we forced another Alexander fumble on their third consecutive possession which Joe Hager recovered. Alexander's day was off to a rough start.

We started our third possession of the game at the twenty-six-yard line. I give South Charleston's defense credit. They had already stopped us twice, and here we were again approaching the end zone. This time, however, they failed to stop us. I scored the game's first touchdown on an eight-yard toss sweep behind blocks from Joe Hager and Brian Bruckner. We ran the play using a new formation South Charleston had not previously seen on film, intentionally creating some confusion for their defense, and once again exemplifying Coach Chmara's ingenuity. We missed the extra point attempt and led 6-0 near the end of the first quarter.

Early in the second quarter, both teams traded punts, and then, unbelievably, South Charleston lost the ball for the fourth time. Starting near midfield, we drove to South Charleston's five-yard line looking to extend our lead. But on the next play, a defender hit Joey just as he tried to pitch the ball to me, and South Charleston recovered the errant toss to stop our most promising drive of the first half.

On South Charleston's next possession, Alexander fumbled for the fifth time in the first half. It may sound like Alexander simply could not hold on to the ball, but our defense forced four of the five turnovers. The first fumble was due to a poor exchange. The next four fumbles were due to hard hits. Despite turning the ball over to us five times in their first six possessions, South Charleston still trailed just 6–0.

After recovering the fifth fumble, we once again turned the ball over on downs. I don't recall ever previously being stopped that many times on fourth down. With the second quarter winding down, Alexander finally broke free for his longest run of the game. Wayne Baumgardner eventually forced him out-of-bounds at our fifteen-yard line. After they picked up a first down inside our five-yard line, our defense held them to a two-yard gain on what I thought was the final play of the first half. However, they managed to call a timeout with three ticks remaining on the scoreboard clock. Time for one more play. We knew Alexander would get the ball. We stopped him just short of the goal in my opinion. Unfortunately, my opinion did not represent the final decision. The officials ruled he had crossed the goal line to tie the game on the final play of the first half. South Charleston missed the extra point, but as luck would have it, we were penalized for being offsides. They converted on their second chance, and we headed to the locker room for halftime, trailing 7–6.

I sat in the locker room in disbelief. *How could this be happening?* We had forced five turnovers and played practically the entire first half on their side of the field, and yet we were losing! Against any other team, we would have been ahead by at least fourteen points. Coach Chmara once again proved to be a calming influence. He put things in a different perspective. He said, "Forget about the score. We outplayed them in the first half. If we continue to outplay them, we will win this game."

That is all I remember from the halftime speech. But I believed him when he said we would win. I always believed him.

We received the kickoff to open the second half. Thus far, South Charleston had prevented us from making any big plays. However, that changed quickly early in the second half as I finally found a seam in the defense for a thirty-two-yard run, putting us once again deep in South Charleston territory. On the next play, we attempted a pass into the end zone, but South Charleston intercepted the throw at the one-yard line.

Despite the interception, we now owned an important advantage in field position, and our defense stepped up to the challenge of holding it. We forced them to punt from the shadow of their end zone. Then, our punt return team came through with a big play as it had done so many times throughout the season. Mark Powell partially blocked the punt, giving us possession of the ball at South Charleston's fifteen-yard line. It took six plays, but ultimately Jaycee Collins plowed into the end zone behind blocks from Brent Sizemore and Robert Lee. We missed the extra point attempt, but we had regained the lead 12–7 late in the third quarter. On South Charleston's next possession, our defense once again limited their offense to three plays and a punt. We took possession of the ball on our twenty-five-yard line and began a drive that carried into the fourth quarter.

As the final quarter began, only twelve minutes on the clock stood between us and the fulfillment of our dream. Seeing the seconds tick off that clock was all that mattered now. We continued our slow but methodical drive. With the championship on the line, we simply kept picking up first downs and letting the clock run, until Jeff Simmons ended the drive with a nine-yard touchdown run behind a great block from Rocky Malamisura. For the extra point attempt, rather than kicking, we ran the option play we often used for two-point conversions. This time I decided to run rather than pass. I outran their defenders to the left corner of the goal line extending our lead to 20–7 about halfway through the fourth quarter. That three-yard run turned out to be my last time carrying the ball as a Bluefield Beaver.

Midway through the fourth quarter, South Charleston had run merely six offensive plays in the second half, and had seen their 7–6 halftime lead evaporate into a 20–7 deficit. Our success in keeping South Charleston's offense off the field played a key role in the game. South Charleston made a couple of first downs on what would prove to be their final possession—one on a fake punt when Alexander simply outran our defensive end, Randy Albert (who has never been allowed to forget that play), and one on a late hit penalty—but we eventually stopped them and took possession of the ball with less than two minutes left in the game. Coach Chmara removed the first team offense from the game and instructed the second team offense to kneel down and run out the clock. When the clock struck zero, we officially joined the great Bluefield teams of the previous decade winning the fifth West Virginia AAA state championship in school history! Coach Chmara's halftime talk turned out to be prophetic.

We celebrated our victory on our field with our fans following the game. It was the first time in my memory that our fans joined us on the field. But this victory entitled us to a special celebration with those who most supported us. We strolled around aimlessly hugging anyone we happened to see. Then, we received our state championship trophy and took the obligatory photos for the next day's front page of the newspaper. The fact my high school football career had just ended did not cross my mind. I would never again suit up in those familiar colors of maroon and white—but what a way to end! The dream I carried into my first day of football practice in August 1973, to win a state championship, had been fulfilled despite it almost dying many times along the way. I finished my high school career with a total of 2,300 rushing yards on 315 carries and scored forty-one touchdowns, twenty-nine of which came in 1975.

For someone who started out as an offensive guard, then moved to fullback, then halfback, then briefly to tight end, and finally back to halfback, my football days over the last ten years had taken many twists and turns, but they ended up as I had always hoped!

The Days That Followed

Following our win, we were honored at several celebrations at school and at local civic events in Bluefield. The championship season bonded our team and our classmates in a way that still exists to this day.

The championship game had been played on the Saturday prior to Thanksgiving. Due to the short school week, our principal, George Erps, dismissed classes after Monday as a reward to the entire school. I spent the rest of that week and weekend hanging out with one of our senior cheerleaders, Karen Noble. Neither of us were dating anyone at the time. Since she was the captain of the cheerleaders, and I often spoke on behalf of the football team, the two of us found ourselves thrown together at many events. I first met Karen at a summer science camp after eighth grade. Karen attended Fairview, the other junior high in Bluefield. Her older sister was a former Miss West Virginia in the USA Junior Miss pageant, and Karen possessed a similar beauty. She and I were good friends throughout high school, but we never dated. That week of Thanksgiving is the only week I spent much time with her. I am glad I have that memory because in May 1978, a mere thirty months later, Karen and her boyfriend were the victims of a double murder which remains unsolved to this day. The tragedy shocked not only our class, but all of Bluefield. Many of our classmates attended her funeral. Some served as pallbearers. As a group, we shared times of extreme highs and extreme lows experienced by few people. The emotional realities of celebrating and mourning with each other united us—those types of experiences will always bind people together.

As the calendar rolled into December, I turned my thoughts to college visits and planning for the next stage of my life. I took six official college visits, the maximum allowed, between December and February. I first visited the University of South Carolina with head coach Jim Carlen, a former WVU coach. South Carolina contacted me early in the recruiting process and accordingly, they were high on my list. However, I was totally unprepared for spending a weekend on a college campus during that first visit. In fact, I had not spent any time contemplating what a typical college weekend would be like. Attending a fraternity party with some college-age students I had met just a couple hours earlier did not interest me, but that is what many of my college visits entailed. After that weekend, South Carolina did not seem like a good fit for me. For this visit, and other visits that followed, I learned the player assigned to host me for the weekend influenced my entire perception of the school. I cannot even remember anything about my host at South Carolina ... other than he liked to party.

When I returned to Bluefield on Sunday, I learned I had been voted runner-up for the Kennedy Award which goes to the most outstanding football player in West Virginia. Prior to then, I did not even know such an award existed. No one at Bluefield ever spoke about it. Robert Alexander, the junior running back we totally contained in the state championship game two weeks earlier, won the award. A couple of weeks later, I was named to the first-team all-state team along with two of my teammates, Joe Hager and Rocky Malamisura. As the calendar crossed into 1976, I began to fully appreciate my high school days were coming to an end. No mandatory winter workouts. No talk of preparing for next season's opening game with my friends. I turned my focus to deciding where I should go to college.

More College Visits

Starting in mid-January, I visited Penn State, Wake Forest, the University of Virginia, Purdue, and Cornell. I admired the winning tradition and aura of Penn State. I enjoyed my visit to State College, Pennsylvania much more than my trip to South Carolina. My host for the weekend showed me a much better time, even though we still hit the Saturday night parties. The coach in charge of my recruitment was Jerry Sandusky, who later became infamous for his actions apart from football. Most football coaches try to come across as tough, but Coach Sandusky came across as light-hearted and jovial despite the fact he coached linebackers at a school known for producing some of the best linebackers in college football. My parents and I also attended a dinner with other recruits at Coach Joe Paterno's home Saturday evening. The thought of playing for Penn State mesmerized me, but Coach Paterno did not offer me a scholarship during my visit. He wanted to wait and see how their other scholarship offers played out before offering one to me. I found that approach to be common. At Wake Forest and Virginia, the coaches exerted pressure on me to sign during my visit because "Other players were on hold." They wanted to determine how many scholarships they had remaining. I enjoyed my visit to Purdue as much as any college I visited, but again, they were not willing to commit. With the signing period closing in, Beattie Feathers of Wake Forest made a trip to Bluefield to get my signature on a letter-of-intent. I was in a constant state of confusion and indecision. With the wisdom of hindsight, my college decision should have been much easier and far less stressful. But at the time, I felt extreme pressure to make the right choice while having no clue what the right choice looked like. I turned down Wake Forest.

With my options narrowing, I decided to sign a letter-of-intent with the University of Virginia. The letter-of-intent served to bind me from signing with another school within the ACC or SEC, but not with another school outside those two conferences. Since no other schools in the ACC or SEC were still under consideration for me, I saw no reason not to sign. I then contacted Jerry Sandusky one last time to see where Penn State stood with respect to its available scholarships. To my shock and surprise, Coach Sandusky responded favorably. He talked to Joe Paterno and they agreed to give me a scholarship for the 1976-1977 season with one caveat. They asked me to agree, with their help and support, to transfer to another college after my freshman year if things did not work out. Jumping ahead slightly, after I had been practicing at Penn State for most of the pre-season camp in 1976, Joe Paterno stopped by my locker and told me he was committing a full scholarship to me for all four years at Penn State. But shortly after that, I decided to transfer anyway.

I signed with Penn State before I made my final visit to Cornell. The coach at the University of Virginia, Dick Bestwick, along with two other coaches and a local UVA grad, Buzzy Wilkinson, all came to my home in Bluefield after I told them of my decision to sign with Penn State. The meeting was quite tense as they put forth several compelling arguments as to why they thought I should attend UVA rather than Penn State. Finally, my mom stepped in and said, "We appreciate you making this trip and we like UVA, but we are going to support Donnie's decision and he wants to go to Penn State." As I said earlier, the entire recruiting process should have been much less stressful.

I enjoyed the last of my six allowed recruiting trips to Cornell in early March. At the time, however, I did not place enough emphasis on the prestige of an Ivy League education. In fact, I knew little about the Ivy League. George Seifert, in his first year as head coach, had led Cornell to a 1–8 record in 1975. Not exactly a great recruiting pitch. But as it turned out, he became a great coach who would later lead the San Francisco Forty-Niners to two Super Bowl championships. Ivy League schools did not give athletic scholarships. Financial aid came in the form of academic or other need-based scholarships. The Cornell coaches told me I could supplement the academic aid I would receive by working an easy, non-demanding job in the library or something similar. One night, I received a call at my home from Ed Marinaro, a Cornell legend and NFL player at the time, who told me I could make plenty of money to pay my out-of-pocket costs at Cornell by house sitting during the summer for Cornell alumni who went on extended summer vacations. He promised to set me up. I considered this enticing offer but decided I should stay committed to Penn State.

Finishing Up

With my college decision finally behind me, I enjoyed the rest of the school year with my family and friends. I continued to gather some end-of-year accolades. I won the Currence Award for Area Athlete of the Year by a sizeable margin. The Currence Award, named after local sportswriter, Stubby Currence, symbolized the most prestigious sports award in the southern West Virginia/southwest Virginia region. Joey Beckett and I shared the Gatherum Award, named for a former team physician, for Bluefield High School athlete of the year. Our track team once again enjoyed some fun out-of-town trips. In late May, we finished in second place at the state championship track meet. One of our defensive backs from the football team, Kelvin Haden, won the 400-meter, 200-meter, and placed second in the 100-meter at the state championship. The person who came in first place in the 100-meter was Robert Alexander of South Charleston. I contributed as a member of the 400-meter and 800-meter relay teams and on the hurdle relays. Finally, I graduated in early June as our class valedictorian.

Filled with a lifetime of memories, my senior year was over. Great coaches, great teammates, great classmates—they all contributed. I could not have asked for more.

Chapter Seven

Playing Defense
College Football, 1976–1979

As I mentioned in the last chapter, I left Penn State in the fall of 1976. At the conclusion of preseason camp, I had earned a starting job on the kickoff and punting teams, thereby proving to myself I could play at the division 1 college level. But after defeating Stanford in our season opener, I decided I no longer wanted to be in State College, PA. It is hard to believe that despite agonizing over my college decision for several months, I now felt like I had made the wrong decision. I sometimes wonder what my life would have been like if I had chosen to remain at Penn State. But each of us make choices throughout our lives and then we must live with our decisions. A couple of years later, Penn State lost the 1978 national championship game to Alabama. It was difficult for me to watch that game, knowing I could have been a part of it. But deep down, I knew I had made the right choice to transfer.

It turned out the right place for me was Wake Forest

University. Yes, the same Wake Forest I came close to signing with in early 1976. I guess some things in life do come full circle. I contacted Coach Chuck Mills at Wake Forest after leaving Penn State and asked him if I could visit him. During the visit in his office, I explained my situation and then awaited his response fully understanding my fate was in his hands at that moment. My future education, teammates, coaches, and friends all hinged on his answer. He told me, "We wanted you last year … and we still want you." Hearing those words from Coach Mills allowed me to breathe a huge sigh of relief. I would be given a second chance.

Although I had been an all-state running back in high school, most colleges, except for Cornell, recruited me as a defensive back. In general, major colleges were not interested in a running back who weighed one-hundred seventy-five pounds. I did not play a single down on offense in college, but I did get to return some kickoffs.

I felt at home at Wake Forest. Wake provided a good mix of academics and athletics. Due to my transfer, I was ineligible to play during the 1977 season. After struggling to a 1–10 record that year, Wake Forest relieved Coach Mills of his head coaching duties. His replacement, John Mackovic, had played quarterback at Wake Forest in the early 1960s as a teammate of Brian Piccolo, who became well-known after the 1971 release of the movie *Brian's Song*, a popular movie about Piccolo's life and death. Coach Mackovic ran a "pass first, run second" offense which was not common during that era.

Prior to the 1978 season, I helped convince Wayne Baumgardner, a sophomore two-way starter as an offensive end and defensive safety on our 1975 state championship team, to attend Wake Forest. Wayne would go on to enjoy an outstanding collegiate career at Wake earning all-ACC honors and setting several Wake Forest receiving records. Wayne became part of a mini pipeline from Bluefield to Wake Forest as Pete Sarver, the quarterback on Bluefield's 1967 state championship team, had helped convince me to attend Wake.

In 1978, I played in all eleven games and started a few games at defensive back. Even though we ended up with another 1–10 record, the season felt quite different from the prior year. We were competitive in most of our games and suffered some close losses including a 13–11 loss to LSU. On a Saturday night at Tiger Stadium in Baton Rouge, I scored my one and only touchdown in college after scoring forty-one touchdowns in high school. Trailing 13–3 late in the fourth quarter, Mark Lancaster, a fellow defensive back, blocked an LSU punt which I scooped up and carried a few short yards into the end zone. We successfully executed a two-point conversion to draw within two points, but we could not stop LSU from running out the clock.

With no one expecting much of us in 1979, Coach Mackovic engineered one of the most remarkable turnarounds in college football history behind a redshirt senior quarterback named Jay Venuto. Jay, in his first year as a starter, proved capable of executing Mackovic's wide-open offense. But Jay did not have to do everything by himself. Our team included several all-ACC and/or future NFL players including James McDougald, Billy Ard, who later won a Super Bowl with the New York Giants, Syd Kitson, Albert Kirby, James Parker, Carlos Bradley, Kenny

Duckett, and the aforementioned Wayne Baumgardner, among others. We posted wins on the road against Georgia, Virginia Tech, and North Carolina and home wins against Appalachian State, East Carolina, Maryland, Auburn, and Duke. Three of those wins came over teams ranked in the Top Twenty at the time. We rose as high as number fourteen in the national rankings before end-of-season losses at Clemson and South Carolina. Nevertheless, we earned Wake Forest's first bowl trip in thirty years and its last one until 1992. Although we lost to LSU in the Tangerine Bowl in Orlando, the 1979 season turned out to be one of the greatest in Wake Forest's football history. It also bookended my football career.

It was time to move on with the rest of my life. After graduating from Wake Forest, I moved to Atlanta, Georgia, and worked for the global CPA firm of Arthur Andersen. In 1982 I met Nancy Ness, a former University of Florida cheerleader and homecoming queen, whom I married in 1983. Nancy and I raised three wonderful children, Keith, Kelly, and Ken, who have their own unique and inspiring stories to tell. Oh, by the way, both Keith and Ken wore jersey number 18 when they played high school football.

Epilogue

My Final Tribute to Coach Chmara

Coach John Chmara passed away on October 28, 2003. During his time as head football coach of Bluefield High School, from 1968 to 1985, he won one hundred thirty games and lost only fifty-three. I was just as proud to play for him in nine of those losses as I was to play for him in twenty-three of his wins. Everyone who played for him would likely say the same.

He helped build, then inherited and maintained a program of excellence during a golden era of Bluefield football history.

To honor his life and legacy, I wrote the following tribute published in the Bluefield Daily Telegraph shortly after his death.

"Unless you had the privilege of playing for Coach Chmara, it is difficult to convey the impact he had on the lives of the young men he coached.

Throughout high school, I never lost the sense of respect and admiration I had for him from the day I first met him. He demanded perfection and would not settle for anything less.

He taught the importance of discipline and preparation ... lessons not only for winning football games, but also for succeeding in life. He could be demanding and tough. He was always fair.

He emphasized sportsmanship and respect for our opponents, but he also instilled in us the belief that we would find a way to win. The motto on the side of our helmet—*We Believe*—was entirely true. He made it true.

Coach Chmara will be remembered for winning championships, but more importantly, he will be remembered and revered for developing the character of champions in the young men he coached.

I, along with numerous others, was certainly blessed to have been able to call him Coach."

About the Author

A native of Bluefield, West Virginia, **DONALD K. JACKSON** has lived most of his adult life in Peachtree City, Georgia, with his wife Nancy, and their three children – Keith, Kelly, and Ken. He is a Magna Cum Laude graduate of Wake Forest University where he lettered in football and received the Atlantic Coast Conference Award for Excellence in Scholarship and Athletics. He remains an avid sports fan.

Made in the USA
Columbia, SC
04 August 2021